John Sturrock was born in Surrey, and educated at the Universities of Oxford and Sussex. A literary journalist, he has since 1967 been a staff member of the *Times Literary Supplement*, and was its Deputy Editor from 1973 to 1984. His books include *The French New Novel* (1969), *Paper Tigers: The ideal fictions of Jorge Luis Borges* (1977) and *Structuralism and Since: From Lévi-Strauss to Derrida* (1980). In addition he has written on French, Spanish and other literary topics for many papers, periodicals and journals in Britain, France and the United States, has worked as a translator, and is the joint editor of the forthcoming *Cambridge Library of Literary Theory*.

JOHN STURROCK

STRUCTURALISM

GENERAL EDITOR
JUSTIN WINTLE

PALADIN
GRAFTON BOOKS
A Division of the Collins Publishing Group

LONDON GLASGOW
TORONTO SYDNEY AUCKLAND

Paladin
Grafton Books
A Division of the Collins Publishing Group
8 Grafton Street, London W1X 3LA

A Paladin Paperback Original 1986

ISBN 0-586-08521-1

Printed and bound in Great Britain by
Collins, Glasgow

Set in Baskerville

CONTENTS

We must therefore be guided by what is common to all. The Logos is common to all, yet the multitude lives as if each had his own intelligence.

Heraclitus

INTRODUCTION

We inhabit a world super-abundantly provided with structures yet which contains remarkably few Structuralists: the proliferation of the one clearly does not entail any large-scale recruitment of the other. Structures are ubiquitous: they are to be found in nature as in culture, in every art and by every science. They may be genetic, anatomical, perceptual, psychological, social, economic, literary, architectural, musical, political or of many other kinds. Everything that is not by its nature indivisible can be shown to have a structure, to be a complex whole capable of analysis into its constituent elements, these elements themselves being related to each other according to rules also to be discovered. It may be the dream of certain sciences to discover ultimately simple entities incapable of further division, but the search for them, as in theoretical physics, is strikingly unsuccessful, since each simple entity that physicists discover turns out on closer acquaintance to be an unsuspected complex one. The indivisible atom of old has failed to be replaced by anything smaller as the presumed 'building-block' of matter. Nor does it seem any longer to make sense to speculate about some ultimate simplicity of substance when substance escapes human observation except in its interdependent motions and effects.

Given the pervasiveness and importance of structures in every field of intellectual inquiry it may seem strange that Structuralists are so few and far between. But the fact is that a great many of those who concern themselves professionally with the study of structures feel no need to call themselves Structuralists nor to advocate something called Structuralism as their preferred method of conducting their researches. Structuralism, unlike structures, is a local phenomenon which has taken root in a small number of intellectual disciplines: in linguistics most influentially, in social anthropology, in history up to a point, in literary studies, in film studies, in psychoanalyis, and in certain branches of philosophy. These are not, very obviously, 'hard' sciences but either 'soft' ones, as in the case of linguistics, or not sciences at all but humanities, as in the case of literary studies. In the 'hard' sciences it may be that structuralism (with a small 's') is obligatory, in so far as it is impossible satisfactorily to pursue a particular science – mathematics, let us say – if one does not do so structurally. This does not apply to the 'soft' sciences or to the humanities. In these, or at any rate in some of them, Structuralism (with a capital 'S') has had to fight to impose itself because it is only one of various methods of inquiry open to those specializing in the subject in question. In a discipline where everyone is willy-nilly a structuralist nothing is to be gained by calling oneself such, whereas in a discipline marked rather by competition between distinctive methods of research and understanding such a declaration of allegiance may be felt essential in order to mark one's own approach off from that of others. Where Structuralism is optional it is also quite often contentious.

It is of importance, therefore, to recognize two aspects to Structuralism; it is both a particular set of ideas applicable in a great many different disciplines and a fairly assertive intellectual movement aiming to persuade those of other allegiances or none that its methods are the soundest and most inspiring on offer in the study of language, history, literature and so on. As a movement localized in time and place, Structuralism deserves the capital letter which it will wear in the present book. It has its ismatic side, without which it could not have survived as the intellectual fashion it has certainly been. Yet as intellectual fashions go it is also an austere one, offering its adepts little opportunity for flamboyance.

Localized or not, it is the intellectual content of Structuralism to which we need to attend, not the personal circumstances or adventures of those thinkers most resoundingly involved with it. There will be no attempts in the body of this book at constructing a history or a sociology of Structuralism, beyond what little may be needed by way of a historical context to clarify and place certain Structuralist ideas. Given which, I will touch briefly here on the when and the where of Structuralism's surprisingly dramatic impact on the intellectual world.

As an academic fashion Structuralism flourished most widely in the 1960s and '70s. In the 1980s its earlier zest and attractiveness have somewhat faded. A number of the more powerful and impressive thinkers associated with it have died; Structuralist ideas now seem less new and subversive than they did; and its authority has been sapped in some quarters by the development of what is known as post-Structuralism (the subject of the last chapter of this study). This does not at all mean that Structuralism is dead, only that many of its ideas have now been accepted outside the Structuralist fold itself into the mainstream of Western thought. The Structuralist revolution, as it was possible once to think of it, has had a lasting effect on the methodology now customary among linguists, anthropologists and others. Nor does post-Structuralism seek to remove or deny Structuralism so much as to purge it of certain failures to live up to its own fundamental insights. Post-Structuralism proves Structuralism, in the old legal sense of the word 'prove'. Structuralism remains richly pertinent as a way of thinking and, for some of us, both fruitful and convincing.

The fashionableness which it enjoyed – and also suffered from – in the 1960s and '70s had much to do with its apparent origination in France. This connection was so close that Structuralism itself has often been referred to as French Structuralism, even though rather few of the ideas it has promoted came to their first fruition in France. Of the main individual sources of those ideas singled out in the pages which follow, one, Ferdinand de Saussure, was Swiss; three, Roman Jakobson, Mikhail Bakhtin and N. Troubetskoy, were Russian; one, Louis Hjelmslev, was Danish; and three, C. S. Peirce, Edward Sapir and Noam Chomsky, were American. Of these, Bakhtin, Jakobson and Chomsky alone were still alive in the years of Structuralism's emergence as a genuine movement. It was only in the retrospect afforded by the sudden new interest in Structuralism that the ideas of these and other precursors were seen to converge in a powerful and important way.

But, to succeed, an intellectual fashion needs living and conspicuous leaders, and if it can find them in Paris so much the better, since it is there that the Western world has long learned to shop for its new ideas. Structuralism became established as a new way of thought thanks to the real or assumed adherence to it of prominent, gifted Parisian thinkers such as Claude Lévi-Strauss, an anthropologist, Michel Foucault, a historian of ideas, Roland Barthes, a literary critic, Louis Althusser, a political scientist, and Jacques Lacan, a psychoanalyst. These five thinkers at no time constituted a school, being far too imperious and, in some cases, vain to endure any such surrender of their individuality. But their ideas unquestionably overlap and came to mark an epoch in contemporary thought. The prestige they enjoyed as individuals in a variety of disciplines was increased by their public's sense that together they were representative of the age, that we live in Structuralist times. The public was right to think that, because it is one of the real strengths of Structuralism that it can call on evidence to support its principles from every known field of intellectual endeavour. It is fair to say, however, that not all of the five thinkers named wished to be thought of as Structuralists, a label they were wary of accepting because of the restrictions it seemed to place on their thought. Lévi-Strauss, the only one of the five to be still active in the mid-1980s, has never wanted to dissociate himself from the Structuralist method, which for him comes close to being a creed and an ethic. It was much less than that for Barthes or for Foucault, who are Structuralists only intermittently and in part. Structuralism is a system of thought which should direct the mind, not coerce it, and there must be room among the ranks of its practitioners for moderates as well as extremists.

It was certainly on the understanding that it was a fresh and invigorating current of thought from France that Structuralism first found a welcome in Britain and in the United States. The home for it, inevitably, was in universities, because Structuralism is essentially an academic movement with few informed followers outside that profession. This relative exclusiveness has had the regrettable effect of making Structuralism appear, first, a more abstruse set of ideas than is actually the case, and second, a more threatening one whenever it is applied in a field where an extreme academicism is especially resented. If, anthropology, Structuralism has made many converts and provoked only relatively benign disputation, elsewhere in academic life, in university departments of Literature, in particular, the same cannot be said. Indeed, the one occasion on which some public notice has been taken of Structuralism in Britain was when a young lecturer in English at Cambridge University was refused tenure because, the allegation ran, he taught English in a Structuralist manner distasteful to his superiors. Whatever the real circumstances of this brief ruction, it serves to show that Structuralism has the capacity to polarize, like any other ism. Once adopted by some – generally the youthful and the iconoclastic – as a rallying-cry or a crusade, it leads instantly to resistance from others. Structuralism is not by its nature provocative, but it may be used, and has been used, to provoke. If anything, its principles should make it unusually tolerant of disagreement, so that the storms it has raised here and there are out of keeping.

The object of the present study is to describe Structuralism, not explicitly to make a case for it. Let it make its own case, on the evidence here provided. The conspectus I am embarking on has surprisingly few predecessors when one reflects on the undoubted impact Structuralism has had in the past twenty years or more.[1] A chief reason why there have not been more introductory volumes of this sort is, I fear, the difficulty of writing one. Structuralism, even of the capital 'S' kind, ranges dauntingly far afield in terms of subject-matter, and to follow it everywhere would be out of the question, except for some unnatural polymath. The only way in which it would be feasible to trace all of its sources and applications would be in the form of a collaborative volume, written by a number of authors competent in a variety of disciplines.

What, then, can a single, less than polymathic author hope to do? To write, as here, a decidedly partial introduction to Structuralism – partial in the sense of being incomplete. This study will touch only on those applications of the Structuralist method which I feel some competence to expound. It begins with Structuralism as a method in the study of language, goes on briefly to its uses in social anthropology, historiography and psychoanalysis, thence to semiotics, seen as the extension of Structuralism to the study of the whole of culture, to literary Structuralism and finally to its most up-to-date avatar in post-Structuralism. I follow this course because it is the course I am equipped to follow, having come to Structuralism by way of its literary and to a rather lesser extent its linguistic manifestations. Another author would certainly want to map the field of Structuralism quite differently. The little book produced under the same title as this one some seventeen years ago by the eminent Swiss psychologist Jean Piaget[2] begins, for example, with a chapter on Structuralism in mathematics and logic, and passes from there to Structuralism in physics and biology. It does not touch at all on semiotics or on Structuralism in literature. That is to ground the subject very firmly and impressively in the 'hard' sciences and thus to claim for it a true universality. By grounding it, as I must, in linguistics, it is still possible to claim universality for it since, just as the system of numbers of which mathematics is made is (or so we hope) universal, so is the abstract underlying system which Structuralist linguists believe is common to all existing and all possible languages. The argument in favour of Structuralism is not weakened necessarily by omitting all reference to its more strictly scientific applications.

The ideal at which any short account of Structuralism aims is itself a Structuralist one: to demonstrate that beneath the superficial variety or diversity of Structuralism's many forms there is an underlying unity, that, for example, literary and anthropological Structuralism have a method and certain crucial principles in common. A formal unity is what has to be demonstrated. This being so, it is easy to see that Structuralism is well placed to help bring about the removal of the boundaries between academic disciplines; it is very much of its age in reinforcing the present healthy and overdue move towards inter-disciplinary study. The Structuralist may seem to those of a narrower, more parochial cast of mind an unwanted intruder, importing alien methods into disciplines proud of having evolved indigenous ones of their own. To others, Structuralism will seem like a genuine opportunity to unify as never before our seriously fragmented understanding of the world around us.

NOTES

1. A bibliography published in 1981 (*French Structuralism*, ed. Joan M. Miller, New York and London) has 5300 entries; of these only 225, very few of them actual books, come under the heading of 'General and Introductory Works'. The remainder are books and articles listed under the names of individual Structuralist thinkers, or specific subject areas that have been affected by Structuralism. Writers on Structuralism have been shy of making the broad comparisons and generalizations the subject badly needs.
2. Jean Piaget, *Le Structuralisme*, Paris, 1968.

1
LANGUAGE

In the course of the present century language has passed from being the transparent, presumedly indifferent medium of thought to being a central and intractable problem of philosophy. We have become aware that what we think is conditional on the structure of the language in which we think, and that no communicable thought is possible independently of language. By giving our attention to the medium it turns out that we are giving our attention to the substance of thought. The formulations we were earlier used to, which implied that thought is 'conveyed' by language, are misleading if they cause us to assume the existence of some 'beyond' of language to which it gives us access. 'All philosophy is "critique of language" . . .' wrote Wittgenstein sixty or more years ago,[1] so helping to inaugurate a philosophical age which has not yet ended and which has elevated the question of meaning – a linguistic question – to be the most important one philosophers can confront. Structuralism, too, is bound up with the nature of meaning and may be seen as a contribution to this seismic shift of philosophical interest.

The extreme claim has been made before now that Structuralism is linguistic or nothing, that it is to be identified with a certain school of linguistics and that when it is applied outside the narrowly linguistic field it investigates its subject-matter, be it historical, anthropological or of some other discipline, as if it were a language. This is a most doubtful analogy which may be discarded at the outset. If I choose to begin this survey of Structuralist method with a chapter on linguistic Structuralism this is because, first of all, language is the central institution of any society and Structuralism is a peculiarly social mode of thought, and, second, because there is no question but that a preponderance of the ideas with which Structuralists in various fields have worked are to be found most clearly formulated in structural linguistics.

There are two distinct strands in structural linguistics, as it has grown since the early 1920s, one European and the other North American. If the European strand has come to be identified with Structuralism then that is because of the French connection alluded to briefly in the Introduction; but the North American structural linguists also evolved certain views about language which converged with those current in Europe, and even where their views appear radically to diverge, the contrast between the two kinds of Structuralism is most instructive. In the pages which follow I shall, where it seems helpful, relate them one to the other. A particular reason for doing this is to counter the diffusionist argument in respect of Structuralism, whereby this school of thought is regarded as having originated in a single centre and then spread to other, receptive intellectual environments around the world. Of course diffusion of ideas is a reality but it is unlikely that they will be intelligently received unless they are found to fit with ideas already prevalent in the environments they have been carried to. The fact that there was a certain Structuralist tradition in the United States well before any invasion of Structuralist notions from Europe helps to explain why these notions were well received and also helps to bear out the case put by Structuralists themselves that Structuralism is a universal and not a local mode of thought, being anchored in the last resort in human biology.

Both in North America and in Europe Structuralism took root in the study of language in the 1920s. In so far as it concerned itself with language in general it marked a revival of a philosophical interest that had very much lapsed in the nineteenth century. With a few remarkable exceptions, such as Wilhelm von Humboldt in Germany, or W. D. Whitney in the United States, nineteenth-century linguists had lost sight of language in their preoccupation with languages. The facts of existing or once existing languages absorbed them, at the expense of the universal language faculty itself: they had no theory of language, that is. Even today many students of language fail to remark the vast difference in scope between the study of language as a universal faculty of our species and the study of actual languages. It is true that the first can be studied only by way of the second and the nineteenth century may certainly claim credit for having assembled many data from actual languages which, once they were systematically compared from language to language, opened the way for the more ambitious and philosophical students to work out a coherent theory of language. Only when such a theory was developed and tested against the plentiful evidence of existing linguistic practice – evidence hugely enriched in this century by the data gathered by anthropologists – could linguistics be said to have a scientific basis.

The founding father of structural linguistics in Europe, and the man frequently looked on as the patron of the whole Structuralist movement, was the Swiss linguist Ferdinand de Saussure. Saussure was born in Geneva in 1857, studied mainly in Germany, taught for a number of years in Paris, then returned to the University of Geneva in 1891 and died there in 1913. He was by training an Indo-Europeanist, a specialist in Sanskrit and its derivative languages, but more speculative than others of his kind; at the age of fifteen, when he already knew French, German, English, Latin and Greek, he produced for one of his teachers an 'Essay on languages' which attempted to derive certain linguistic universals from phonetic patterns he believed to be common to several of the languages he had met with.' This proto-Structuralist exercise was judged presumptuous by its addressee. But at the age of only twenty-one he published in Leipzig a celebrated 'Dissertation on the primitive vowel-system in Indo-European languages' whose method is certainly Structuralist. The object of this essay was to study the various forms taken by the so-called 'Indo-European *a*', but as the work proceeded Saussure came to appreciate that the question was a wider one than he had foreseen, and that to study one vowel meant studying them all. In the words of the Dissertation's preface: 'it is clear that in fact it is the system of vowels as a whole that falls within the radius of our observation and whose name must be inscribed on the first page.'[2]

In his lifetime Saussure published very little, but in his later years of teaching he had moved from his special concerns with Indo-European or Germanic languages and given courses of lectures at Geneva in General Linguistics. In 1916, three years after his death, two of his former students published under his name a *Course in General Linguistics*. This was a text constructed by themselves from their collation of sets of notes taken by a number of students who had attended Saussure's lectures. In the seventy years since then the *Course* has made its way around the world, quickly in a few countries but with extreme slowness in others – the first English translation was not made until 1959.[3] An attentive reading of this, for its time, revolutionary text remains the best introduction there is to the principles on which Structuralism rests. The fact that the text is not the work of Saussure himself but of his students or followers is unimportant, since the soundness or otherwise of the ideas which the text expounds is not dependent on our knowing whether they are given in precisely the form Saussure himself would have wanted. Their worth may be determined without any certainty as to their authorship. I shall use Saussure's name throughout my own text as if he were, unequivocally, the author of the *Course*, although his uncertain relationship to that book bears interestingly, as we shall see, on the issues raised by Structuralism.

Like any other innovator Saussure was in reaction against an orthodoxy: in his case the orthodoxy of the later nineteenth century which dictated that language be studied historically and genetically. The questions that linguists then chose to ask and to answer were chiefly ones of the origins and evolution of particular languages or groups of languages. They were obsessed with change and ignored what it was exactly that was changing. The first great shift which Saussure introduces into his linguistics is intended to go against this emphasis and, as it were, to hold the object of study – language – steady for long enough to enable its permanent structure to be investigated. 'Properly conceived of,' Humboldt had declared, 'language is something persistent and in every instant transitory.'[4] It was the persistent aspect which Saussure meant to uncover.

A language may be studied along two axes, one temporal and the other, in a manner of speaking, spatial. These two axes Saussure named the diachronic and the synchronic. A diachronic linguist studies a language as it changes through time while a synchronic linguist studies it statically, in its given state at a particular moment of time. The premise of the synchronist is that the capacity of a language to alter unceasingly may be set aside for the sake of studying its more or less permanent constitution. The study of language itself, as the hypothetical template of all existing languages, is essentially a synchronic one because it is searching for the constants of language. The structures which Structuralists look for endure, which is not to say that they never change or last for ever. Structures too evolve, except perhaps at that extreme level of abstraction where one believes one has identified the basic constituents without which it could not *be* a structure.

Saussure draws the vital distinction between the two contrasted axes of study in these terms:

> Synchronic linguistics will be concerned with logical and psychological connexions between coexisting items constituting a system, as perceived by the same collective consciousness.
> Diachronic linguistics on the other hand will be concerned with connexions between sequences of items not perceived by the same collective consciousness, which replace one another without themselves constituting a system.[5]

One of the oddities of the *Course in General Linguistics*, given the influence it has had, is that it nowhere contains the term 'structure'. But 'system', as it occurs in the quotation above, will do well enough instead. A system, like a structure, is formed of elements which coexist; it cannot be formed of elements which are successive. It may today seem a relatively trivial stipulation that language be studied as a system, but that is only because we have become so accustomed to the synchronic point of view. In Saussure's time it was not a trivial stipulation because it went against the grain among linguists, who resisted the abstraction which it involved of language from history.

The systematic, synchronic perspective opens the way for language-study to be saved from an unambitious atomism, or mere accumulation of linguistic facts, which may be associated with one another but never fully correlated. Structuralism begins on the far side of such limitations as these. As will repeatedly become clear in the present study, it seeks to comprehend linguistic facts as elements in a single system, and it is the profound shift of perspective from the diachronic to the synchronic that enables it to do so. This integration of the linguist's proper subject-matter is located by Saussure, be it noted, within the 'collective consciousness', which is an abstraction, since it is not commensurate with the consciousness of any given individual, however massively knowledgeable or competent in his native language. Language, in the Structuralist sense, is most emphatically an abstract object. It is also the possession of society, which is another name for the 'collective consciousness', never the possession of an individual.

Having laid down the first principle of linguistic Structuralism, which will serve very well as the first principle of Structuralism *tout court*, it will be as well now to look across at American Structuralism, which was equally committed to the synchronic point of view. But in its earlier stages it was also bound to a largely descriptive and behaviourist account of language. The most energetic practitioners of it had no truck with speculation of Saussure's sort, believing that the truth about language would be found, if at all, only at the conclusion of a mighty effort to identify and classify all existing linguistic forms. Leonard Bloomfield, whose 1933 book on *Language* was as influential among linguists in America and Britain as Saussure's *Course* was in Europe, refused to see it as any part of his mandate to move beyond the description of languages to generalization about them:

> The only useful generalisations about language are inductive generalizations. Features which we think ought to be universal may be absent from the very next language that becomes accessible . . . The fact that some features are, at any rate, widespread, is worthy of notice and calls for an explanation; when we have adequate data about many languages, we shall have to return to the problem of general grammar and to explain these similarities and divergences, but this study, when it comes, will be not speculative but inductive.[6]

This is Anglo-Saxon empiricism at its most stringent; not until all the facts are in is it worth advancing a theory. (That empiricism is itself a theory, and as such determines which linguistic facts are relevant to the inquiry and which are not, is an admission commonplace enough today, but certainly not in Bloomfield's day.) Bloomfieldian linguistics is often referred to as 'distributional', its aim being to establish a full description of all the contexts in which the various categories of words can be found in everyday usage. Its achievements are thus broadly normative and statistical. What Bloomfield calls the 'fundamental assumption of linguistics' is '*that in every speech-community some utterances are alike in form and meaning*' (Bloomfield's italics).[7] This is the minimalist programme of a linguist who believed that the proper study of language should be conducted without concern for 'ideas' or for human consciousness, collective or otherwise. Language was a certain kind of physical event in the world, a response to stimuli from the environment, and its structures, accordingly, were all on the surface, being the sum total of all known grammatical practices.

One very striking difference between American Structuralism and the Saussurean kind is brought out by Bloomfield's equation of the study of language with the study of grammar. The *Course in General Linguistics* has remarkably little to say about grammar, to which Saussure seems not fully to have turned his mind at the time when he gave the lectures on which the book is based. Where Bloomfield and the other American Structuralists see grammar as the central feature of language, Saussure chooses to see rather its power of signification. In a review of the *Course* published in 1923 Bloomfield stresses this divergence: 'In detail, I should differ from de Saussure chiefly in basing my analysis on the sentence rather than on the word.'[8] And so it has remained: American Structuralism is concerned with syntax, Saussurean Structuralism with the verbal sign or word. Syntactic structures have the advantage of being more conspicuous than the highly abstract structures Saussure finds in language, since syntax *is* structure, being a conventional arrangement, varying from language to language, whereby words enter into various formal relations with one another. We hear syntax when spoken to and see it when we read. Its structures are conspicuous because they are on the surface of language, a point I shall come back to when turning to the contribution made by Noam Chomsky to Structuralism.

Before that, however, another of Saussure's cardinal distinctions must be brought in: that between *langue* and *parole* or, as they are usually given in English, 'language' and 'speech'.[9] This distinction follows on from that between the synchronic and diachronic axes of language-study: *langue* is the term Saussure gives to the 'system' or totality of language stored in the 'collective consciousness'. The grammar of the language, obviously, makes up a large part of that system, which also includes the full vocabulary or lexicon of the language. The *langue* thus comprises a full catalogue of the elements of a language together with the rules for their combination. *Parole* on the other hand is the use which individuals make of the total resources of the language they are born into. It is actual utterance, in speech or in writing. If *langue* is a structure then *parole* is an event. The first is an abstraction, the second is real. Without the events there would be no way in which we could know of or investigate the structure, and without the structure the event would be formless and without meaning: the two are wholly interdependent.

The contrast between *langue* and *parole* is one which extends everywhere in Structuralism, sometimes expressed in a more modern way as the contrast between the 'code' and the 'message' (although it can be misleading to equate the language-system with a 'code' when it is characterized by being primary and open to all, rather than secondary, like most codes, and restricted in its use). It is, before all else, a contrast between the collective and the individual. This is a contrast of which Structuralism makes much, championing as it is bound to do the collective at the expense of the individual. For Saussure the *langue* is a social bond:

> It is a fund accumulated by the members of the community through the practice of speech, a grammatical system existing potentially in every brain, or more exactly in the brains of a group of individuals; for the language is never complete in any single individual, but exists perfectly only in the collectivity.[10]

The fact that a language is a structure which is realized only partially and imperfectly in those who use it raises the key problem of the articulation of *langue* with *parole* or system with event. How is it that the system comes to be sufficiently represented in our brains so that we can, without being at all aware of it, exploit it in our daily use of language? This is not a problem Saussure himself faces up to but it is one which has been placed at the heart of contemporary linguistics by Chomsky. Chomsky would certainly not wish to be thought of as a Structuralist because his career as a linguist has been spent in vigorous and fruitful reaction against the Structuralism of Bloomfield and others in America. But he may be claimed for Structuralism because Chomskyan linguistics is structural through and through and bears importantly on some of the issues raised by Saussure.[11]

Like Saussure, Chomsky strives to go beyond the data available to him from everyday language-use, to construct a theory of, in his case, grammar. He has elaborated a practice of linguistics which he declares to be 'qualitatively' different from the Structuralism that prevailed among American linguists in his young days – a Structuralism which collected facts and classified them, but forbore to interpret them theoretically. Because it was behaviouristic in its outlook – fanatically so in the case of Bloomfield – it regarded the individual's use of language as habitual: in Bloomfield's words, as 'a composite result of what he has heard other people say'.[12] (The word 'composite' there begs all the interesting questions which Chomsky was to raise.) According to this model of *parole* we know what to say because we have listened to other people and can proceed either by repetition or by 'analogy' with what we have heard in similar circumstances. Bloomfieldian linguistics calls for the complete elimination of 'mind' and its replacement by a peculiarly extensive notion of 'habit', as if we were, as language-users, incapable of doing more than respond to the situations we find ourselves in.

Chomsky has worked to restore 'mind' to linguistics by showing how starkly a model such as Bloomfield's fails to account for the infinite creativity of our language-use. He argues that we are constantly producing sentences in our language which we have never heard before, which may not be closely conditional on the circumstances in which they are uttered, and which cannot be accounted for by any weak concept like 'analogy'. Language, that is, is far more than habit and could never be satisfactorily acquired in childhood on the behaviourist model of stimulus and learned response.

To account for the acquisition of language is for Chomsky

the greatest challenge open to the structural linguist. No one questions that there are structures in language – surface structures are apparent in our syntax; or that to use language successfully demonstrates a command of these, though we might be quite unable to offer any description of the syntactical rules we are observing every time we speak or write. But these surface structures are not enough, Chomsky suggests, because sometimes they are ambiguous or capable of more than one meaningful interpretation. This is the clue to another level of linguistic structure, the 'deep structures' to which Chomsky has over the years given a certain celebrity, though he no longer likes the term 'deep' in view of its unwanted connotations of profundity. The 'deep structures' are not ambiguous, they are open to only one semantic interpretation, and they are turned into surface structures by the rules of what Chomsky calls a 'transformational' or 'generative' grammar. These transformations are, in his phrase, 'structure-dependent . . . in the sense that they apply to a string of words by virtue of the organisation of these words into phrases.'[13] That is to say that the transformation depends on the syntactical organization. The sentence 'Mary has lived in Princeton' is transformed into the interrogative 'Has Mary lived in Princeton?' by, in Chomskyan terms, interchanging a noun phrase ('Mary') with the first element of the auxiliary ('has'). According to Chomsky no human language allows of any such transformations except in this 'structure-dependent' fashion.

There is no need here to go into the form that these transformational rules take, or the manner in which they operate: Chomskyan grammar is not a pursuit for the lay person because it soon grows algebraic and extremely complex. What concerns us, in this conspectus of Structuralist ideas in linguistics, is the close connection between Chomsky's proposed model of language acquisition and Saussure's distinction between the language-system and everyday language events.

It is tempting to equate Saussure's pair of terms, *langue*

and *parole*, with the pair which Chomsky introduced to mark his own distinction between system and event: 'competence' and 'performance'. One can see at a glance, however, that there is a significant difference between Saussure's *langue* and Chomsky's 'competence', in that where the first is specified as something belonging to society or the language-community, the second remains the possession of the individual. Saussure more or less ignores the question of how the individual acquires a mastery of the essentially collective system, whereas Chomsky tackles it very directly. In order to explain the fact of the individual's linguistic creativity he posits a 'tacit knowledge' of the language-system as a whole, an 'internalized' grammar which enables each of us to generate a potentially infinite number of new sentences. Between the stimulus and the response of the old behaviourist model, or the 'input' and 'output' of subsequent, computer-influenced models, Chomsky inserts his own intermediary in the form of an innate mental structure specific to humankind. This structure alone can answer the otherwise insoluble question of how we can each have a considerable, if never a complete mastery of the *langue*:

> Specifically, we must ask how, on the basis of the limited data available to him, the child is able to construct a grammar of the sort that we are led to ascribe to him, with its particular choice and arrangement of rules and with the restrictive principles of application of such rules. What, in other words, must be the internal structure of a learning model that can duplicate this achievement? Evidently, we must try to characterise innate structure in such a way as to meet two kinds of empirical conditions. First, we must attribute to the organism, as an innate property, a structure rich enough to account for the fact that the postulated grammar is acquired on the basis of the given conditions of access to data; second, we must not attribute to the organism a structure so rich as to be incompatible with the known diversity of languages. We cannot attribute knowledge of English to the child as an innate property, because we know that he can learn Japanese as well as English. We cannot attribute to him merely the ability to form associations, or to apply the analytical procedures of structural

linguistics, because ... the structures they yield are not those that we must postulate as generative grammars.[14]

Chomsky's innate mental structure has met with strong objections in its time, especially when it has been reformulated as the language-user's 'tacit knowledge' of his language, since knowledge that is tacit, and which most of us would be incapable of making explicit under any conditions, seems like a luxury, even granting Chomsky the distinction philosophers recognize between 'knowing-that' and 'knowing-how'. (As a hypothesis, such a 'knowledge' of language is susceptible of the perplexing question put by Wittgenstein: 'Suppose it were asked: "*When* do you know how to play chess? All the time? or just while you are making a move? And the *whole* of chess during each move? How queer that knowing how to play chess should take such a short time, and a game so much longer!"'[15]) However, by insisting on the need for a structural 'competence' to make sense of the facts of language-use, Chomsky brought to the study of language a dynamism and a popularity it would otherwise have lacked. His version of Structuralism has considerable implications for the view that we take of human capacities, as well as strengthening the belief common to all versions of Structuralism that the human mind is Structuralist because it cannot be anything else, that the structures it finds in what it analyses match in some sense innate mental structures, in a pattern reminiscent of Leibniz's 'pre-established harmony'. Chomsky, indeed, has used the term 'pre-set' to describe the mind of the human infant in its first exposure to the language of its community, meaning that it is biologically fitted to acquire any language at all and that the acquisition of a particular language thus represents a restriction of its capacity, not a growth.

Chomsky has followed in the tradition of American Structuralism in taking the sentence to be the basic unit of language and in showing relatively little interest in the word. With Saussurean Structuralism the reverse is the case. Following the example of Saussure himself, it has fixed its attention on the word in its function as linguistic *sign*. The definition of language offered by a Saussurean Structuralist would be that it is a system formed of linguistic signs, and for the sake of argument we can say that the terms 'word' and 'sign' are here interchangeable.[16]

If signs, however, are the basic elements of the language system, they are not *simple* elements. Language, by any definition, is a correlation of sounds with meanings and in Saussure's analysis of the linguistic sign this correlation is paramount. He analyses the sign into two aspects or faces: a phonetic or acoustic aspect and a semantic one. The sign is both sound and sense – though one needs to be careful in using terms such as 'phonetic', 'acoustic' or 'sound' since these apply to signs only in their spoken form; in their written form they need be neither pronounced nor heard. Given which caveat – it will return in full force in the last chapter of this book, on post-Structuralism – I shall continue to follow Saussure in characterizing the twin aspects of the sign as acoustic and conceptual. *Both* these aspects, be it noted, are mental, for the good reason that they are indissoluble; the sign is a unity and its two aspects exist in total dependence one on the other. Sound without sense is not a part of language, it is, in the telling description found by modern theorists of communication, mere 'noise'; and sense without sound (or without its material manifestation as writing) is impossible.

For the two aspects of the sign Saussure found the terms *signifiant* and *signifié* or, as they are usually translated into English, 'signifier' and 'signified'.[17] This terminological complex of Sign, Signifier and Signified is perhaps Saussure's most influential gift to Structuralism, providing as it does the wherewithal to analyse the process of signification and to distinguish readily between the manifest and the abstract faces of the sign. Once it has been successfully understood, this distinction provides an unrivalled tool in linguistic as well as literary and other kinds of textual

14

analysis. Struggling, indeed, to decide what it was that all those thinkers labelled in the popular mind as Structuralists might have in common, Roland Barthes concluded that it was 'probably the serious resort to the lexicon of signification . . . look to see who uses signifier and signified, synchrony and diachrony, and you will know whether the structuralist view of things has taken shape.'[18] The word 'serious' is worth stressing here, since not all resorts to Saussure's lexicon qualify as that.

The Saussurean sign, then, is an abstract object, it is not to be confused with whatever it is the sign of, with something in the world. This something is what philosophers know as the *referent*. Structuralists do not always keep hold as they should of the distinction between the conceptual aspect of the sign, or signified, and the referent, and remarkably, Saussure himself appears to confuse them in the text of the *Course*. The first principle which he lays down there concerning the linguistic sign is that it is 'arbitrary', by which he means that its form is not determined or 'motivated' by the thing it is the sign of, or referent. The proof of this is the enormous variety of signs to be found in different languages for the same referent, from which one can conclude that these signs could have taken a different form from that which they in fact have; though it has to be realized that the arbitrariness of the signs of our language does not set us free to change them: they are arbitrary but also fixed, by a consensus which has accrued over the centuries of a language's history and which we are powerless as individuals to change. A demonstration of arbitrariness is the fact that the animal which on one side of the English Channel is referred to as *horse* is referred to as *cheval* on the other side. These are two signs with a common referent, but we cannot and must not conclude from that that they are two signifiers with a common signified, because the signified of *horse* is to be found in the 'collective consciousness' of the English language-community and the signified of *cheval* in that of the

French language-community; neither signified is to be found standing in a field.

Grave misunderstandings of the nature of Structuralism follow if signifieds and referents are taken to be synonymous, as they are at one point in the text of the *Course in General Linguistics*, where one can read that 'the signified "ox" has as its signifier *boeuf* on one side of the frontier, but *Ochs* on the other side'.[19] This mis-statement of the case, which contradicts the very terminology Saussure has himself introduced, is typical of many similar ones made since by others. In Saussure's case, the confusion can certainly be put down to the way in which the text of the *Course* was constructed by its editors, collating material dating from different stages in the evolution of his ideas,[20] but in the case of others who have repeated the same error, we have evidence of something else, which is the considerable difficulty we all face in preserving the conceptual aspect of the sign as an abstraction indissociable from its complementary acoustic or graphic aspect. We are led into error by a certain idealism, whereby we dissociate the two aspects of the sign and take the conceptual aspect to have precedence over the acoustic or graphic aspect. Many people assume that signifieds pre-exist signifiers, or that meanings 'await' expression. The effect of that assumption is to assimilate the signifieds, stored up as they must be in some pre-verbal repository, to the infinite number of potential referents in the world, which undeniably do pre-exist their human investment by language. This is a question that comes very much to the fore in post-Structuralism and in the work of Jacques Derrida, and I shall return to it at the appropriate point.

The 'arbitrariness' of the linguistic sign is a more radical matter than is sometimes realized, because it establishes the autonomy of language in respect of reality. Natural languages differ very markedly from each other not only in their vocabulary, as in the case of *boeuf* and *Ochs*, but also in their grammatical structure. The Structuralist point of view in language is fundamentally opposed to that old but still quite popular conception of language which sees it as a nomenclature, or a conventional item-by-item naming of the contents of the world around us. It is possible to argue plausibly that a language is a nomenclature only for as long as one restricts the inventory of things waiting to be named to straightforward categories of physical objects or actions. If a language were all nouns and verbs, the argument might hold. But because languages contain other categories of sign, and because the signs enter into complex logical relations with one another when they are used, the nomenclature argument becomes wholly inadequate.

Structuralism tends to reverse the precedence which a nomenclaturist accords to the world outside language, by proposing that far from the world determining the order of our language, our language determines the order of the world. Because no two languages order the world in quite the same way – a disparity soon appreciated by anyone who tries to translate from one language into another – no two language-communities can understand the world in quite the same way. This profound consequence of 'arbitrariness' is neatly summed up by John Passmore in the dictum, 'Languages differ by differentiating differently'.[21] This is the prime lesson to be learned from all the comparative work done on languages in the period which preceded Structuralism and of the linguistic field-work done by anthropologists in cultures strikingly different from their own. American structural linguistics relied heavily on the great deal that had been learned of the grammatical structure of American-Indian languages, which often strikes an English mind as most eccentric, because the formal relations which it chooses to express are not those we are used to. Structuralism of this comparative kind does not presuppose that any one linguistic structure is superior to any other, only that all are greatly or slightly different from one another. There is no 'master' structure by which to evaluate other, 'lesser' or more 'primitive' structures. In the words of the first great American linguist, to whom Saussure paid due tribute:

There are no relations to which a language must necessarily give expression; there are only certain ones which are more naturally suggested, of which the expression is more practically valuable than others: and what these are, we can learn only from the general study of languages; our own educated preferences are no trustworthy guide to them.[22]

Whitney here maintains a relativism more extreme than that of other structural linguists, who would not concede that 'there are no relations to which a language must give expression'. Edward Sapir, for example, whose views generally come closest among the earlier school of American Structuralists to those of Saussure, holds that certain of the relations expressed in grammatical structure are 'essential' and therefore presumably universal:

If I wish to communicate an intelligible idea about a farmer, a duckling, and the act of killing ... I can find no way of dodging the issue as to who is doing the killing. There is no known language that can or does dodge it, any more than it succeeds in saying something without the use of symbols for the concrete concepts.[23]

Whether or no the relational categories of agent and action are universal, as Sapir claims them to be, one can say that what *is* universal is the need for relations, or for a structure. There can be no language or thought that is not structural.

It is possible and tempting to posit, beyond any structure, an inaccessible and undifferentiated process in the human mind of which language is the manifestation and to which it actually *gives* a structure. Saussure makes this assumption:

Psychologically, setting aside its expression in words, our thought is simply a vague, shapeless mass. Philosophers and linguists have always agreed that were it not for signs, we should be incapable of differentiating any two ideas in a clear and constant way. In itself thought is like a swirling cloud, where no shape is intrinsically determinate. No ideas are established in advance, and nothing is distinct, before the introduction of linguistic structure.[24]

It is rash to strive to reach, by means of metaphors, beyond language in this way, when by doing so *in* language one can produce only a paradox: a systematic or structural formulation of the supposedly formless. However, the hypothesis of a formless substratum, of thought as somehow opposed to language, or to the communicable ideas which represent the articulation of thought, enables one at least to take a dynamic view of linguistic structure. In this model, language has something *to* structure, and the term 'structure' itself enters service as a verb and leads us on to the notion, dear to some Structuralists, of *structuration* (the basic faculty of the human intelligence according to Piaget).

The remarkable degree of autonomy which language enjoys in respect of reality follows from its systematic nature. We should think of the language-system as being applicable to reality as a whole instead of in its separable elements. To conceive of it as the sum of very many one-to-one correspondences of words and world is to misconceive it utterly. The form taken by the constituent elements of the system is determined not by their referents, as we have seen, but by the place they occupy within the system. Each element is, as Saussure insists, 'a form, not a substance'.[25] This is perhaps hard to grasp, but it is the radical consequence of the 'arbitrariness' of signs and of language as a whole. Signs are forms because they determine one another, as fellow members of the one integral system. It is their place within the system which decides what Saussure calls their 'value', which he is careful to distinguish from their 'signification'. This latter term he reserves for the actual application of a sign to the world, in an act of reference; it is a relation between language and reality. The 'value' of a sign, on the other hand, is an internal relation, depending as it does on that sign's multiple relations with other signs of the language.

Saussure is here practising very obviously a linguistics of the word, and not the sentence, but his assertion that the linguistic sign is essentially a form rather than a substance can be corroborated from Sapir, who was certainly a linguist of the sentence and of grammar. For Sapir too, 'The word is merely a form, a definitely molded entity that takes in as much or as little of the conceptual material of the whole thought as the genius of the language cares to allow.'[26] In this instance the 'whole thought' – and Sapir does not ask how that can ever be abstracted from the actual forms of its expression – plays the same role as the undifferentiated flux of 'thought' in general plays for Saussure, as what is somehow there to be articulated in whatever form a particular language permits. Sapir's is the attitude of a comparatist, for whom the comparison between different languages is a matter of considering their different formal structures; Saussure is looking beyond the characteristics of existing linguistic structures to the structure of structure itself, to what makes language possible.

The notion of a sign's 'value' leads up to the more embracing notion of a language as a system of differences. No sign is sufficient unto itself: it is what it is, linguistically, by virtue of what it isn't. If it is an 'entity' at all, then it is a negative entity, differential in its nature as well as in its function:

> In the language itself, there are only differences. Even more important than that is the fact that, although in general a difference presupposes positive terms between which the difference holds, in a language there are only differences, *and no positive terms*. Whether we take the signifier or the signified, the language includes neither ideas nor sounds existing prior to the linguistic system, but only conceptual and phonetic differences arising out of that system. In a sign, what matters more than any idea or sound associated with it is what other signs surround it.[27]

The differential nature of the sign in both its aspects, as sound and as sense, is no impediment to the positive *use* of signs; their differential nature is then eclipsed inasmuch as there is no need for us to be aware of it. Again, one might say that where the system is of a negative, differential nature (though it has been argued against Saussure, notably by Roman Jakobson, that grammatical categories cannot be understood in this differential way), linguistic events are positive. Saussure adopts the analogy (in strikingly similar terms to those later found by Wittgenstein) with the game of chess, games being ideal examples of rule-bound structures. A piece in chess falls under the category of pawn or bishop not by virtue of what it is independently of the game, which is a carved bit of wood or ivory, but by virtue of the value invested in it by the rules of chess and by the differentiation of pawns from knights from queens and so on. We may not be conscious of this differentiality every time we move a chess piece, but it is very clear that such an 'event' is wholly determined by the structure of the game in which it occurs. The analogy is especially helpful in demonstrating the crucial difference between form and substance, given the insignificance, for someone actually playing chess, of the substantiality of the pieces. In the same way, for someone actually using language, the linguistic substance, which may be of interest to a physiologist or a graphologist, according to whether it is the spoken or the written substance, is of no account, since what the language-user is using is the *forms* of his or her language.

The signs of a language thus become subject to the so-called 'play of differences', a concept popular among post-Structuralists. Because they are mere forms, signs have neither complete stability nor complete identity. Change in one sign will entail changes in those other signs with which it enters into relations in the system, and this is true whether the changes are to the sound of the sign or to its meaning. Changes in a language are of course a diachronic factor, not a synchronic one, but they do not affect the systematic nature of language itself; the synchronic point of view of Structuralism does not at all deny the influence of outside factors working to bring about changes in the grammatical, phonetic or semantic structure of a language, it only insists that these changes themselves be seen as 'structure-dependent', that, as Sapir has it, the 'drift' which a particular language displays in its evolution through time is conditioned by the structure of the language and 'constituted by the unconscious selection on the part of its speakers of those individual variations that are cumulative in some special direction'.[28] It is a fact, also, that although the entry into a language of new forms belongs to the diachronic or historical study of that language, when this happens the new forms do not replace old ones straight away; there is sure to be a period when new and old forms coexist and compete until one or other gives way, or until both are preserved and accorded different 'values' in order that they may be differently used. During this period of coexistence linguistic change becomes a synchronic study: indeed, an especially telling example of what linguistic coexistence implies since where a new form and an old compete the differences in 'value' between them may be particularly subtle.

Saussure's recognition that the signs of a language have a 'value' as well as a 'signification' brings in for the first time the 'semiotic' function of language (the term derives from the Greek word *semeion* meaning 'sign'). Semiotics is the subject of the third chapter of this book and I will not linger over it here except to say that it concerns itself with signs such as those of which a language consists in so far as these belong to a system: with *how* they mean rather than with *what* they mean. Semiotics may thus be contrasted with semantics, which concerns itself with the 'signification' of signs or the use we make of them to refer. Semiotics has to do with the word as a unit, semantics with words combined in sentences: 'In semantics the "meaning" results from the sequence, appropriateness and adaptation of the different signs among themselves. That is absolutely unpredictable. It opens out on to the world. Whereas in semiotics meaning is turned in on itself and as it were contained within itself.'[29] As a semiotic item a linguistic sign may be differentiated from others of its kind both by sound and by sense. The English sign *horse*, for example, is defined phonetically by the fact that it resembles but is not identical with *hearse*, *coarse*, *whores*, *house*, and so on through a long list of such near homophones (including the actual homophone *hoarse*, from which it is not differentiated phonetically at all but will usually be so semantically by the meaning of the sentence in which it is used). Should the pronunciation or inscription of a sign depart far enough from the norm to render it phonetically or graphically indistinguishable from those adjacent to it in sound or appearance, then, obviously, only the context can disambiguate it. But as an abstract item of the language such identity as a particular sign commands is secured by the small phonetic or graphic differences between it and neighbouring items.

Its conceptual 'value' is rather harder to determine because here we are quick to lose sight of a sign's 'value' in the face of its common 'signification'; its positive use in an act of reference prevents us from attending to its constituent differentiality. A comparison between different languages is often the simplest way in which to demonstrate how semantic 'values' function. The example which Saussure himself provides involves the English word *sheep* and the French word *mouton*, which are two signs used alike to refer to the one animal. But if they are identical in signification they are not so in 'value', because the English language contains another sign *mutton* to go alongside *lamb*, to refer to sheep when they are eaten. The French language has no equivalent, but uses the one term *mouton* to refer to both the living animal and its meat. Hence the incompatibility between the 'values' of the two terms in the two languages, since English in this instance offers a contrast or relation absent from French. There will be more to be said on this matter of structural semantics at a later point; suffice it for now to emphasize that any sign in any sign-system has a 'value' by virtue of belonging to that system.

A sign's 'value' becomes especially apparent when it is one of several alternatives which might be substituted for one another in an act of reference; thus the 'value' of *horse* is made more apparent by the existence in English of such other signs as *nag*, *mount*, *pony*, *steed* and the like, all of which might be chosen to refer to an actual horse and all of which clearly possess meanings additional to the mere 'horse-ness' of the creature in question. These additional meanings are the sign's 'connotations', of which there will be more to be said when we turn to the matter of semiotics. The question of a sign's semantic 'value' brings us up against the encyclopedic nature of the semantic structure of a language, which is a network so rich in relations between terms that it will perhaps always defeat analysis.

The systematic nature of language introduces into its use what might be called a 'vertical' dimension, since each sign which finds its way into an actual utterance, in speech or in writing, invokes, potentially, all the other signs to which it bears a relation. This dimension of language Saussure calls the 'associative' and he contrasts it to the other, 'horizontal' dimension of language: the linear or 'syntagmatic' one. Since Saussure's own time, the associative dimension has come more and more to be known as the 'paradigmatic', which makes it sound more formal than what Saussure appears to have had in mind, since many of the associations which particular signs carry for those who use them may be private and thus less than paradigmatic, if by this term we mean sets of substitutable signs common to the whole language-community. However, Saussure's insistence that language works in both dimensions simultaneously marks him off once again from the grammatical tradition of American Structuralism, which is concerned more or less exclusively with the syntagmatic dimension of language.

The contrast which Saussure makes is between the actually uttered and the unuttered, or, once again, the language-event and the language-system. The multiple associations of which signs are simply the node are not to be identified with the language-system in its entirety, but they are as it were the living proof that such a system exists, and that one sign leads inescapably to another. This conception introduces the notion of *absence* into the account of language: 'Syntagmatic relations hold *in praesentia*. They hold between two or more terms co-present in a sequence. Associative relations, on the other hand, hold *in absentia*. They hold between terms constituting a mnemonic group.'[30] These 'absent' associations with which most if not all of the linguistic signs we use are invested may of course be brought to presence and inserted into a syntagma – this process is the one which, Jakobson argues, characterizes the 'poetic' use of language as opposed to the everyday use (see the chapter on Literary Structuralism). Students of language are perhaps entitled to leave it out of account, as they mostly have done, on the grounds that what is 'absent' is a wasteful distraction from the problems posed by what is present. But there is a less creditable reason also for this neglect of the associative dimension of language-use, which is the fear we may feel at discovering how influential it is. Many of us like to think that when we use language we control it more or less totally and that it is we who determine the sequence of words or thoughts each time we write or speak; we are not happy to allow that language itself can prove more powerful than we are and that the associations of the signs we have already used may be determining the choice of the signs to come. This loss of authority in the 'speaking subject' or language-user is a most important and contentious aspect of Structuralism, exploited to the full in post-Structuralism as I shall hope to show, and it can be traced back to this insistence of Saussure that the language-system impinges at every moment on language-events.

If it is possible to codify all the syntagmatic associations of signs – this is what American 'distributionalist' grammarians sought to do – the same is not true for their paradigmatic associations. '[An] associate group has no particular number of items in it; nor do they occur in any particular order,' declares Saussure.[31] The most one can do is to divide them into the two necessary classes of phonetic and semantic associations, while hoping that there is not a third class, peculiar to linguists, of grammatical associations. The phonetic associations of a given sign such as *horse* might eventually be listed, starting with those I have already suggested and pursuing the catalogue ever further from the sign with which one began. A similar catalogue for the semantic associations of the same sign is out of the question, for the reasons I have indicated, that there is no end to them and no definitive or commonly agreed order in which they can be placed. Phonetic associations are impersonal, being determined by the phonetic structure of the language (some people are much more alert to them than others, naturally, and could produce longer lists of valid associations) but semantic ones allow for an infinitely greater freedom, even if in the end they too must be bounded by the semantic structure of the language because what lies outside that is literally inconceivable. All that Saussure himself will say of the 'associative relations' of a sign is that they form a 'constellation'.[32]

I have already pointed to the fact that the word 'structure' occurs nowhere in the *Course*. It was indeed not until some twelve years after that book was first published that European Structuralism may be said to have begun as a distinctive school of linguistic thought. The occasion for the first true airing of the term 'structure' in the sense we now give it was a conference of linguists held at The Hague in 1928, and the branch of linguistics it was then applied to was phonetics. The innovators were three Russian linguists working outside Russia: Roman Jakobson, S. Karčevsky and N. Troubetskoy, whose base was Prague. Prague Structuralism, which was innovative in the fields both of language and literature, and of art in general, and which survived in Czechoslovakia even after its early leaders had either died or left the country, is a most important if rather neglected tributary to the stock of doctrines which have come to constitute Structuralism.

In 1929, the year after their intervention at The Hague,

these three linguists published, in French and anonymously, their so-called *Theses*, or manifesto, whose overall title proclaimed their affiliation with Saussure: 'Problems of method stemming from the conception of language as a system'. The system they were concerned with was one on which Saussure had had relatively little to say, though what he did say was impeccably Structuralist: the phonetic or phonological system of language. The method which the Prague linguists intended to follow was to 'characterize the phonological system by necessarily specifying the relations existing between the phonemes, that is, by tracing the plan of the structure of the language under consideration'[33] – a method which they declared could be followed equally fruitfully in studying other systems of the language. Henceforward the study of language could be explicitly Structuralist.

Saussure had foreseen that the study of the sound aspect of language needed to be carefully divided into the study of the production of sounds and the study of their reception. Merely as sounds they are a subject for physiology, which can take up questions of how the speech organs function. But as the sounds *of a language*, in the ear of a user of that language, they become a subject for the linguist, who can investigate their nature as participants in a language's sound-system. Phonetics may be left to study the physiological side of sound-production, phonology turns instead to the analysis of the sound-system. It is with phonology that Structuralism is concerned.

The units out of which the sound-system of a language is formed had been discovered many years before the Prague Structuralists produced their manifesto: they are the 'phonemes' of the language, which might be defined as the smallest distinctive units of sound that a language possesses. They are the sounds which tell different words apart. Thus, in English *p* and *b* are separate phonemes because *pill* and *bill* are separate words; similarly, *i* and *u* are separate phonemes because *pill* and *pull* are separate words, and *l* and *t* because *pill* and *pit* are separate words.

Phonemes must be found by a test of substitution, usually known as 'commutation', whereby changes are induced in the phonetic make-up of the word in order to see at what point it becomes a different word. Phonology thus has to start from the semantic aspect of a sign, or the signified, which determines the permissible extent of phonetic variation in a sign before it turns into a different sign. The test is one of sense, not sound.

Each language has its own phonological system, recognizing differences which other languages may not recognize. Jakobson gives as a telling example of this the fact that whereas in English *r* and *l* are distinct phonemes – *rash* and *lash* are distinct English words – in Korean they are not, so that a speaker of Korean can substitute one sound for the other without any loss of sense, hence the regularity with which, when learning English, a Korean speaker may substitute *l* for *r* unaware that he has now to deal not with mere sounds but with phonemes.[34]

The number of phonemes in any given language is unexpectedly small, a fact which makes the phonological system a particularly good model for the systematicity of language as a whole since with a restricted number of elements it is able to generate an enormous number of different signs. In this respect phonemes may be compared with words, whose possible meaningful combinations are certainly innumerable, bearing out the cardinal principle common to Saussurean and Chomskyan Structuralism that language is a structure characterized by a 'constructivity without limit'.[35]

The phonological Structuralism developed in Prague had as one of its main purposes to *integrate* the phonetic data which had been collected over the years and classified but never grasped as the manifestation of a single abstract scheme, applicable to any language whatsoever. The new Structuralists had higher aims, founded on their conviction that, in Troubetskoy's words: 'A phonological system is not the mechanical sum of isolated phonemes, but an organic whole whose members are phonemes and whose structure is subject to laws.'[36]

But what the Prague Structuralists did not at first have was a systematic and meaningful way of relating phonemes adequately one to the other. Saussure had written of the 'oppositive' nature of phonemes, thereby assimilating them to the other elements of language, but it is not clear how phonemes can be held to be 'opposed' one to another; they differ from each other but difference is not necessarily a relation of opposition. The discovery in phonology which remained to be made was that phonemes could be analysed, they were not the indivisible atoms ('symbolic atoms' Sapir called them) earlier linguists had imagined them to be. During the 1930s, and chiefly by Jakobson, phonemes, first vowels and then consonants, were further broken down into 'distinctive features'. This deeper analysis established new relations between phonemes according to whether, for example, they were 'voiced' or 'unvoiced', 'nasalized' or 'not nasalized', etc. By such means English *b* can be shown to stand to English *p* in a relation of voiced to unvoiced, as does English *d* to English *t*. If one then asks whether this means that one or other pair of consonants are the voiced and unvoiced versions of the 'same' phoneme, the answer is 'no', they are not the voiced and unvoiced versions of anything. They are the two terms of a relation and that is all: opposed phonemes are an ideal example of Structuralism's denial of self-sufficient entities. The analysis of phonemes into distinctive features also represents a further economy for the linguist inasmuch as there are even fewer distinctive features at work in a particular language than there are phonemes – Jakobson allows five only for the sound-system of French, and three among the eight vocalic phonemes of Turkish.

The establishment of this underlying phonological system of 'distinctive features' achieves an ultimate segmentation of a language's sound-system, and lends a new rigour and weight to Structuralism's dependence on pairs of opposed terms, already adumbrated by Saussure. As Jakobson claims: 'The oppositions of such differential qualities are real binary oppositions as defined in logic, i.e., they are such that each of the terms of the opposition *necessarily* implies its opposite.'[37] Thus 'voiced' and 'unvoiced', or 'nasalized' and 'not nasalized' are pairs of terms allowing of no middle term between them, the second example showing very usefully that in such a system the absence of a feature is equally as significant as its presence.

'Distinctive features' are the furthest point it is possible to reach in the analysis of language without leaving the language-system for that of the human anatomy. Such terms as 'voiced' and 'unvoiced' look to be drawn from the mechanics of sound production, except that the distinction between them is an acoustic one on which depends our understanding of what we hear. (The analysis of the elements of the written language, or 'graphemes', could presumably be conducted in similar terms to those used in the analysis of phonemes, and the 'distinctive features' of written signs be codified. However, no adequate report seems to exist of research conducted along such lines.)

One needs to be clear, finally, that phonology occupies itself with the study of *langue* and not of *parole*. The phoneme is an abstraction, not an actually uttered sound: 'The phoneme is not to be identified with the sound, yet nor is it external to the sound; it is necessarily present in the sound, being both inherent in it and superposed upon it: it is what remains invariant behind the variations.'[38] In Saussurean terms we can say that the phonological system of our language is 'internalized' in our brains, or in Chomskyan terms that it is 'acquired', even though we are seldom or never conscious of it when speaking. 'Distinctive features' are a fact of the linguist's analysis and not of the consciousness of speakers, though we receive indications of the sound-system of language whenever we meet with error in hearing or speaking and one phoneme is mistakenly exchanged for another. The phonological system of a language is a cultural phenomenon, not a natural one: it represents indeed the point where nature becomes culture, or where the continuum of naturally produced 'noise' is articulated into the discontinuous and distinct sounds of significant speech. Structuralist phonology is the bridge between linguistics and the sociological uses of Structuralism, which are the subject of the next chapter.

NOTES

1. Ludwig Wittgenstein, *Tractatus Logico-Philosophicus*, p. 63.
2. Ferdinand de Saussure, *Cours de Linguistique Générale*, ed. Tullio de Mauro, p. 327.
3. The first English version of the *Cours* was made by Wade Baskin and published in both Britain and America in 1959. A second, improved translation, made by Oxford's (first-ever!) Professor of General Linguistics, Roy Harris, was published in 1983. This second translation is the one I have used in the present book from which to quote, with one important terminological departure – see Note 17 to the present chapter.
4. W. von Humboldt, *Linguistic Variability and Intellectual Development*, trans. G. C. Buck and F. A. Raven, p. 27.
5. Saussure, op. cit., p. 98.
6. Leonard Bloomfield, *Language*, p. 20.
7. *Ibid.*, p. 78.
8. *A Leonard Bloomfield Anthology*, ed. C. F. Hockett, p. 107.
9. In his introduction to his translation of the *Cours* Roy Harris makes some interesting remarks on the difficulty of translating the term *langue* into a single English term suitable for all its uses in French (pp. xv–xvi). 'Language' and 'speech', as the equivalents of Saussure's *langue* and *parole*, leave a lot to be desired. The important thing to remember is that this pair of terms stand to one another in the relation of 'system' or 'abstract structure' to 'concrete event'.
10. Saussure, op. cit., p. 13.
11. For a useful survey of Chomsky's references to and judgements on Saussure, see Tullio de Mauro's edition of the *Cours*, pp. 400–404.
12. Bloomfield, op. cit., p. 46.
13. N. Chomsky, *Language and Mind*, p. 61.
14. *Ibid.*, p. 170.
15. L. Wittgenstein, *Philosophical Investigations*, p. 50.
16. Signs and words should not be equated, since there are signs in a language-system which are not words (marks of punctuation, for instance). If a sign is a 'unit of meaning', it

is clear that parts of words can also be counted as signs, since parts of words can mean in isolation from the rest of the word. Prefixes and suffixes, for example, bear meaning and occur in dictionaries as independent units. To define what exactly a 'word' is is extremely difficult. I do not attempt it.

17. In his translation of the *Cours*, Roy Harris translates *signifiant* and *signifié* as 'signal' and 'signification' respectively. This is a break with the (admittedly short) tradition in English of translating them as 'signifier' and 'signified'. Harris does not justify this novelty and I have chosen in the present book to reverse it where quoting from his translation. The terms 'signifier' and 'signified' seem to me to have the advantage over those suggested by Harris of strangeness and of having been created for the actual purpose of analysing a linguistic or other sign. The contrast between them is stronger than that between 'signal' and 'signification', which are terms familiar from other contexts and therefore liable, I believe, to produce confusion.

18. R. Barthes, *Essais critiques*, p. 214.

19. Saussure, op. cit., p. 68.

20. It is well worth reading Tullio de Mauro's note on this question in his edition of Saussure, pp. 442–3.

21. J. Passmore, *Recent Philosophers*, p. 24.

22. W. D. Whitney, *Life and Growth of Language*, p. 221.

23. E. Sapir, *Language*, p. 94.

24. Saussure, op. cit., p. 110.

25. *Ibid.*, p. 111.

26. Sapir, op. cit., p. 32.

27. Saussure, op. cit., p. 118.

28. Sapir, op. cit., p. 155.

29. E. Benveniste, *Problèmes de Linguistique générale Tome 2*, p. 21.

30. Saussure, op. cit., p. 122.

31. *Ibid.*, p. 124.

32. *Ibid.*

33. See E. Benveniste, *Problèmes de Linguistique générale Tome 1*, p. 94.

34. R. Jakobson, *Six Lectures on Sound and Meaning*, trans. J. Mepham, p. 31.

35. See *Edward Sapir: Appraisals of his Life and Work*, ed. K. Koerner, p. 77.

36. Benveniste, op. cit., p. 95.

37. Jakobson, op. cit., p. 81.

38. *Ibid.*, p. 85.

2
SOCIAL SCIENCES

From the time in the late 1920s and early 1930s when Structuralism first distinguished itself as a method of integrating and explaining the data of phonology, its originators believed that, as Structuralists, they were falling into line with a mode of thought characteristic of the age. Structuralism was an idea whose time had come and a part of a widespread reaction against the modes of thought that had preceded it, which might variously be called atomistic, empiricist or behaviouristic. Those scholars and thinkers with whom Structuralists were in the sharpest disagreement had tended to treat their data as self-contained facts, and the gathering of those facts as an end in itself. They had paid too little attention to the relation of fact to fact within the systems of which the facts could pertinently be taken to be members. If the empiricists advanced underlying theories to account for their data, they were unambitious ones, and some refused to be thought of as theorists at all: Zellig S. Harris, a central figure in American structural linguistics, and a teacher of Chomsky, was especially notorious for disclaiming any theoretical as opposed to a descriptive intention in his linguistic researches.

The early Structuralists sensed that empiricism of this unadventurous stamp was on the retreat, and that the way was open for a more speculative cast of mind to replace it. Writing in 1933 the phonologist Troubetskoy who, like his fellow exile from Russia, Jakobson, was a man of wide and various cultural and scientific interests, associated the revolution he was helping to bring about in the study of

language with the general direction of contemporary Western thought:

> Present-day phonology is characterised above all by its struc-
> turalism and its systematic universalism ... the age in which
> we live is characterised by the tendency of all scientific disci-
> plines to replace atomism by structuralism and individualism
> by universalism (in the philosophical sense of those terms, of
> course). This tendency may be observed in physics, chemistry,
> biology, psychology, economics etc. Present-day phonology is
> not isolated therefore. It forms part of a wider scientific
> movement.[1]

Like any other new mode of thought Structuralism was
not a total and unheralded innovation but a confluence of
ideas prevalent already in the intellectual world of Western
Europe. It would be perverse to set out here to trace which
Structuralist thesis might have come from where; perverse
because that would be to revert to the pre-Structuralist
obsession with evolution and with the genesis instead of
the form of ideas. Structuralism teaches, on the contrary,
the joyful dethronement of what the French political philosopher Louis Althusser sardonically calls 'the Gods of
Origins and Ends'.[2] This is a warning not, as Structuralism's opponents like to interpret it, against pursuing any
form of diachronic inquiry whatsoever, but against the
common fallacy that any system can finally be explained in
terms either of its origins or of its ultimate destination.

However, the better to describe Structuralist thought,
now that we are passing from its linguistic manifestations
to those in other disciplines where it has been especially
influential, it will help to refer briefly to two currents of
ideas which were strongly formative on the minds of
linguists such as Jakobson and Troubetskoy. These two
currents are those of phenomenology and of Gestalt
psychology.

Phenomenology is a school of philosophical thought
which flourished in Germany, chiefly in the work of Husserl
and of his pupil Heidegger, and was later popularized up

to a point in France, in the abundant writings of Sartre and those of Merleau-Ponty. It has remained little studied and even less admired by Anglo-Saxon philosophers. a neglect that may well be a contributory factor to the resistance subsequently shown to Structuralism itself, which is dependent in important ways on certain of phenomenology's insights.

Phenomenology was one of the periodic attempts made by philosophers to re-establish their discipline on absolutely certain foundations, to make it, that is to say, a science to which all rational persons must accede. Phenomenology's ambitions, which have not been realized, were to free philosophical thought from the preconceptions which lead even philosophers astray when they consider ultimate questions of perception, sensation, knowledge and so on. It was an attempt at the accurate description of consciousness, and at removing once and for all the ancient division practised by so much philosophy of the subject from the object of human thought. Phenomenology takes subject and object to constitute a whole, and the relation between one and the other to be 'intentional'. The objects of our thought are 'intended' by ourselves in different ways, of perceiving, imagining, remembering, etc. As phenomenologists like to repeat: consciousness is always consciousness *of* something, it is a whole divisible only falsely into an independent subject and object. In consequence everything in consciousness is meaningful, it being the function of consciousness to synthesize the flow of human experience into intelligible structures.

Phenomenology is a form of philosophy and not of psychology, it seeks to describe the essence of consciousness and not consciousness as it functions in this or that individual. The question which exercised Husserl was how truths such as those of logic and mathematics, which are not psychological truths, can be known by individual minds: 'Our problem now concerns precisely the ideal objects which are thematic in geometry: how does geometrical ideality (just like that of all sciences) proceed from its primary intrapersonal origin, where it is a structure within the conscious space of the first inventor's soul, to its ideal objectivity?'[3]

In Structuralist terms the issue is that of the articulation of system with event. Husserl's answer to the question posed above is that geometrical ideality proceeds from its 'source' within the individual by means of language, which objectifies it and makes it an inter- instead of an intrapersonal truth. Phenomenology is a true ally of Structuralism in equating the 'world' with everything that can be said or written.

It is a true ally, too, in drawing so absolute a distinction between the variables of consciousness, which are of no account, and the invariant or structural features of it, which it is philosophy's task to identify. Husserl takes the age-old problem of the nature of our perception of the external world, in order to clarify the phenomenological method:

> For instance, the phenomenology of perception of bodies will not be (simply) a report on the factually occurring perceptions or those to be expected; rather it will be the presentation of invariant structural systems without which perception of a body and a synthetically concordant multiplicity of perceptions of one and the same body as such would be unthinkable.[4]

There is evidence, even in this brief example, of how phenomenology takes an active view of human consciousness: in perceiving we *organize* our environment, and in our capacity for retention, or memory, we synthesize present and past. It would not be going too far to say that consciousness is a 'structuring' faculty of human- and, presumably, animalkind.

Like Structuralism after it, phenomenology declared itself to be a method and not a doctrine. A crucial part of its method involved what is generally called a 'bracketing' of the world in its actual uniqueness, which we experience in every moment of our conscious lives. That uniqueness has to be set on one side because it cannot be part of philosophy, it is entirely subjective and psychological. The experiences in which the phenomenologist deals are thus *examples* of these other, unique experiences; they are real experiences in their inter-personal or communicable aspect. Here the closeness of phenomenology to Structuralism is very apparent. Words and sentences too, as items in the objective language-system, are essences, they cannot represent the uniqueness of the experiences we use them to describe. Moreover, in its autonomy, language also may be said to 'bracket' the living reality of things, inasmuch as we can use it freely without concern for its truthfulness. Just as the phenomenologist is as interested in the structure of imagining as in that of perceiving, so the structural linguist can proceed without ever asking himself which linguistic structures are used to say true things about the world and which to say untrue or wrong things.

The second large-scale and widely influential movement in contemporary thought which lent weight to Structuralism was Gestalt psychology which, like phenomenology, was German in origin and flourished over much the same period, between 1910 and the 1930s. *Gestalt* is the German word meaning 'pattern' and the essence of Gestalt psychology is the claim that all conscious experience is patterned. Gestalt psychology, again like phenomenology, deals in wholes; it runs counter to the beliefs of behaviourism in psychology, which studied isolated episodes of human behaviour in terms of stimulus and response – one stimulus producing one response. The Gestalt psychologists argued, on the contrary, that such simplicity was a misrepresentation of how human beings perceive and respond to their environment:

> Our view will be that, instead of reacting to local stimuli by local and mutually independent events, the organism responds to the *pattern* of stimuli to which it is exposed; and that this answer is a unitary process, a functional whole, which gives, in

experience, a sensory scene rather than a mosaic of local sensations.[5]

Wolfgang Köhler, the author of these words, had himself been trained first as a physicist and brought with him into psychology the physicist's notion of the physical 'field' or delimitable whole within which may be observed a dynamic interplay of forces following certain paths and obeying certain laws. An intervention from outside the 'field' disturbs the equilibrium of this system, whose readjustment will be not purely local but general and systematic. Similarly with the 'field' of human consciousness, which is constantly being called upon to readjust itself faced with stimuli from the external environment. Gestalt thought is system-bound once again and studies not independent entities but the relations between terms. (In the quotation from Köhler which I have given, his contrast between a 'sensory scene' and a 'mosaic' of local sensations is an unhappy one, since a mosaic is itself a work of art and as such an example of an organized whole or structure.) The finding of Gestalt psychology is that we make sense of our environment contextually, by differentiating its elements one from the other. To revert to the term Saussure introduced, the 'value' of a particular element, let us say a colour that we perceive, is determined by the presence of other, different colours; it has no 'absolute' value independent of the context in which we perceive it.

Along with phenomenology, then, Gestalt psychology encourages the view that the function of the human mind is either to recognize structures in whatever it turns its attention to or else to project structures into whatever it attends to. There can be no mental experience which is not organized and no mental entity conceivable independently of the others with which it enters into relations. We remember structurally just as we perceive structurally. The suggestion made by Köhler and others is that Structuralism is inscribed in our bodies because of the manner in which the central nervous system works. The structures of experience reflect bodily structures or, as Köhler briefly puts it, 'units in experience go with functional units in the underlying physiological processes'.[6] Thus does Nature make Structuralists of us all. Two structures functioning in parallel, as proposed by Köhler, can be described as 'isomorphic' or of like form, and when it comes in Structuralism to relating one structure to another, so as to determine their relations, the concept of isomorphism clearly has a large part to play. The ultimate Structuralist dream (or fantasy) might be of the discovery of a Structure of Structures which would enable us to claim that all structures were isomorphic of one another.

The Structuralist thinker who has acknowledged most roundly the affiliation between his own ideas and those of Gestalt psychology is the anthropologist Claude Lévi-Strauss, who also takes it for granted that Structuralism is the one appropriate mode of thought or intellectual method for the present age. He is the most purely Structuralist thinker of all, having not only put Structuralist methods to work in his professional field of social anthropology but also drawn sweeping philosophical conclusions from what he regards as their unquestioned success about the nature of the human mind. He looks on his achievement as convergent with those of others, working in the physical or the human sciences, and as a contribution to the general study of organization.

The study of (normally) an alien society, which is what social anthropologists engage in, offers particular advantages to Structuralism. In the first place, an alien society is neither altogether familiar nor altogether unfamiliar; it is a human organization certain to share some of its rules, customs and beliefs with other societies and certain also to possess some rules, customs and beliefs peculiar to itself. It shows both sameness and difference when it is compared with other societies. Second, a society is essentially a synchronic system, to be studied in its present configuration: in this it is exactly the same as a language as Saussure defines it. It is unnecessary, and may indeed be extremely misleading, for a social anthropologist to attempt to explain his findings in genetic or historical terms, when the appropriate explanation of what he observes in the course of his work in the field is clearly the synchronic one, which explains any particular practice in terms of what it means here and now and not in terms of how it originated. The anthropologist needs to take account of the history of the people he studies – always supposing it has a history, in the form of authenticated documentary records – only to the extent that the people's understanding of its own history plays a part in its life today. The synchronic point of view necessarily presides in anthropology.

A third reason why Structuralism lends itself so well to the requirements of social anthropologists is that it is in fact nothing new for them, since they have traditionally set out not simply to describe social structures but also to explain them, to produce working models of human collectivities. A society without a structure that is perceptible to the observer, who is himself presumed to enjoy the benefit of being uninvolved personally in that structure, would be quite unintelligible, a random collection of data proving nothing. There are no doubt accounts of societies which purport to be purely empiricist, but it would be good to be told which facts about a given society the empiricist observer chooses to record and what order he then assembles them in. An anthropological fact only becomes so once it has been recorded: it is an *account* by an observer of something observed and conveyed, usually, in a language other than that of the society under study.

It would not be unreasonable, I hope, to describe much social anthropology done before Lévi-Strauss came on to the scene in the 1940s as proto-Structuralist. Structuralism as advocated and practised by Lévi-Strauss since that time has met with suspicion and sometimes hostility, particularly from anthropologists trained in the empiricist tradition of Anglo-American anthropology. This is mainly because Lévi-Strauss's Structuralism claims to explain so much and to explain it so logically, to the point where he proffers it as a theory of culture, which to many anthropologists is to go far beyond the evidence acquired. Where the empiricist tradition accumulates data which seem to confirm the endless diversity of social practices, between one society and another, Lévi-Strauss claims that the same data can be used, in ever more abstract ways, to reveal the fundamental unity of all cultures. He represents Structuralism in its most extreme will to universalism.

Yet there is much common ground between Lévi-Straussian Structuralism and the theoretical anthropology which preceded it, especially that branch of it known as 'functionalism'. Functionalism, too, is tied to the synchronic point of view, seeking as it does to explain the practices it comes across in terms of their everyday social function. Each practice is a part whose 'value' lies in the place it can be shown to occupy within the whole, and that is simple Structuralism. Anthropology above all cannot afford to worry itself about the vagaries or eccentricities of individual behaviour because it must remain scrupulously restricted to the collective. It seeks the systematic sets of rules on which a society's collective behaviour ultimately rests, and may ignore those defections or transgressions which are merely individual. Thus an empiricist anthropologist like A. R. Radcliffe-Brown is every bit as severe a Structuralist as Lévi-Strauss in writing that: 'So also the social phenomena which we observe in any human society are not the immediate result of the nature of individual human beings, but are the results of the social structure by which they are united.'[7]

Such a forthright dismissal of the individual as a proper subject of anthropological study brings out very well the opposition of Structuralism to all attempts at a psychological explanation of the data which it collects. Lévi-Strauss himself carries this anti-individualism to excessive lengths (I will come back to this), but this is not incumbent on all Structuralists. Structuralism cannot register phenomena that are unclassifiable but it may still esteem them; in this it is no different from any other scientific method.

The great difference between Lévi-Strauss's Structuralism and the rototypes of Structuralism that preceded it in anthropology lies in their respective scopes. A structuralist such as Radcliffe-Brown studies structures which are markedly less abstract than those pursued by Lévi-Strauss. Families, schools, churches are all social structures and may all be described with a certain degree of abstraction in order to bring out how they function and what the relations are between their members. Such a description will be structuralist but hardly Structuralist, because Structuralism has wider ambitions and cannot rest until it has integrated a whole range of seemingly confused and confusing evidence of this kind into a single model. Lévi-Strauss has greatly enlarged the scope of social anthropology and made it a much more intriguing discipline for outsiders in doing so. By seeking to integrate the cultural practices of a people with their social, economic and political practices he has opened the subject up. Where once the lay reader might have been bored and bemused by technical accounts of, let us say, Australian aboriginal kinship structures, he is at once attracted by the suggestion that those structures can be assimilated to the forms observable in aboriginal rock-art; and it is in arguing for assimilations of this kind that Lévi-Strauss has made his name. The dramatic enlargement of the proper field for anthropological study is wittily summarized in Ernest Gellner's contrast: 'Structure was, for instance, whom one could marry; culture was what the bride wore.'[8] Thanks to Lévi-Strauss and the Structuralism he has so widely imposed, culture has come to seem a matter fully deserving of intelligent and systematic investigation.

Gellner's remark, which is not I think meant to be flattering to Lévi-Strauss, brings out something especially valuable in Structuralism, which is its great openness to data, however trivial they may previously have been thought to be. To a traditional anthropologist a bride's costume may well have seemed an entirely negligible matter, whereas the marriage-rules observed in her union

were of lasting importance. But when it is faithfully practised, Structuralism works against any condescending
assumption that some aspects of social behaviour are
insignificant, because its principles force it to take an
interest in everything or, if that is a superhuman ambition,
at least to treat everything it meets with as interesting
because significant. Brides' costumes are something better
discussed under the heading of Semiotics (see Chapter 3),
but suffice it for now to point out that they are never
merely functional. There is more to a bride's costume in
any society than keeping her warm or simply covered; its
colour, shape, decoration and material all either follow or
in some cases break certain norms, and it is perfectly
feasible for an anthropologist to construct a model whereby
to explain the various clothing practices observable in a
given society.

The aim of Lévi-Strauss's Structuralism is to make all
such manifestations of culture intelligible. It is his belief
that they are evidence of an unconscious logic whose actual
forms will necessarily vary between one society and another
but which is, in its fundamental structure, common to all
humanity. As an anthropologist he has proceeded, therefore, in just the same way as a comparative linguist must,
on the assumption that however much one language may
vary from another there is a fundamental structure common
to them all, an essence without which no language could
be a language.

The influence of structural linguistics on Lévi-Strauss
has indeed been unusually direct. In the winter of 1942 he,
an exile from occupied France, found himself in New York
and lecturing at the same institution as Jakobson, an exile
now from occupied Prague. Listening to what Jakobson
had to say about phonology, and in particular about the
analysis of phonemes into opposed pairs of 'distinctive
features', helped greatly to set Lévi-Strauss on the path
towards his mature Structuralism. He had already found,
during his field-work among Brazilian Indians, how reliant
anthropology is on language as it sets about gathering

information from native informants and how hard it is for the anthropologist accurately to notate a wholly alien language. The lesson he learned from the new phonology was one of reducing confusion and multiplicity to order: 'What I was to learn from structural linguistics was . . . that instead of losing one's way among the multitude of different terms the important thing is to consider the simpler and more intelligible relations by which they are interconnected.'[9] To which acknowledgement one might add that the binarism which is so marked a feature of Lévi-Strauss's Structuralism is also to be found in Jakobson's phonological scheme, which, as I have indicated, represented an advance on earlier formulations because it sets the distinctive features of which phonemes are composed into relations of opposition one with another. The schemata which Lévi-Strauss employs in his brilliant exercises in social and cultural interpretation rely exclusively on such binary pairs of terms or concepts, even though he is prepared to allow that some of the oppositions he believes to be endemic in social and cultural organization are weaker than others.

Lévi-Strauss was especially interested in the notion of the phoneme as the basic element of language because he saw it as the point where nature joined with culture, and the opposition between nature and culture had already struck him as the crucial one which we must recognize and chart if we are to understand what is specifically human in human life. Greatly influenced by Marx, Lévi-Strauss has that thinker's obsessive awareness that everything that is social or cultural is man-made and might therefore be remade. The truly natural is by definition unintelligible, but the cultural, which is a departure from the natural, *is* intelligible and thus capable of being integrated within some systematic explanation. In linguistics the phoneme is as near as we can come to nature while remaining cultural, because a phoneme is an element in a social institution and therefore no longer a natural sound. It is, above all, a meaningful sound.

Lévi-Strauss believed that he could provide an ingenious parallel for the phoneme from the anthropological world, and that was the 'incest taboo' or proscription of sexual relations with near kinsfolk which he assumes to be common to all societies. The incest taboo is for Lévi-Strauss the point at which culture takes over from nature, or from mere biology, leading as it does to marriage outside the immediate family group and to the institution of a 'network of exchange' in which the items offered for exchange are women. The network so founded becomes a means of 'communication' between human groups and it is through communication that the transformations on which Lévi-Strauss's model of society relies so heavily can take place, when one group 'communicates' its myths, rituals, customs and goods to another. In the process of passing from group to group, or population to population, these myths etc. undergo changes, since the group receiving them will inevitably seek to assimilate them to the existing cultural stock and to its own natural environment if need be.

The parallel between the linguist's phoneme and the incest taboo is not one which has always impressed Lévi-Strauss's fellow anthropologists, depending as it does on treating sexual relations and marriage as if they were synonymous; but it is no part of my commission here to report on quarrels internal to social anthropology. What is important is that Lévi-Strauss went on to practise anthropology in the strong conviction that structural phonology is a model fit to be followed and to be adapted for use in the study of such traditional anthropological questions as kinship. Kinship lends itself well to his methods because it is bound up with terminology, or with the names which various societies choose to give to various degrees of family relationship and descent. A kinship system may thus be looked on as a 'language':

Like phonemes, kinship terms are elements of meaning; like phonemes, they acquire meaning only if they are integrated into systems. 'Kinship systems', like 'phonetic systems', are built by the mind on the level of unconscious thought. Finally, the recurrence of kinship patterns, marriage rules, similar prescribed attitudes between certain types of relatives, and so forth, in scattered regions of the globe and in fundamentally different societies, leads us to believe that, in the case of kinship as well as linguistics, the observable phenomena result from the action of laws which are general but implicit.[10]

It is thus the task of the Structuralist in anthropology, as in other fields, to make the empirical be also the logical, to achieve what Lévi-Strauss calls a 'concrete logic'. The individuals within the societies which anthropology studies have little or no explicit knowledge of the kinship system which regulates certain of their dealings with one another. That system is 'unconscious' until it is brought into consciousness by the anthropologist. The Structuralist thus grasps the system from outside and not from within. In a further comparison commonly made between the methods of social anthropology and of linguistics, the outside view which reveals the logic of particular social practices is known as the 'emic' view, and this is contrasted with the inside, empirical or 'etic' view – these two terms having been borrowed from the similarly contrasted 'phonetic' and 'phonemic' approaches to the sounds of language, where the first is descriptive and the second analytical. The Structuralist is 'emic' or nothing; indeed, Lévi-Strauss has gone so far as to claim that in linguistics the 'etic' or purely empirical level does not exist; he uses the findings of the Russian psychologist A. R. Luria to argue that our brains analyse phonemes into their distinctive features in the very act of hearing them. This is further proof for him that we cannot but be Structuralists.[11]

The Structuralist study of kinship tends towards an algebra of diverse though structurally coherent systems of terms and attitudes; as such it is of scant interest for laypeople. The same does not hold, however, for those other key topics of social anthropology to which Lévi-Strauss has applied his method: to totemism, ritual, myth and art. It helps to realize that in seeking to integrate the study of all these various social practices so as to prove their common logic, Lévi-Strauss is being polemical. In particular, he is challenging the old but still prevalent supposition among Western anthropologists and citizens generally that the peoples whom anthropology studies are simple-minded, to the point even where they may come to seem different in kind from ourselves. There is a generosity in Lévi-Strauss's lifelong efforts to raise the standing of indigenous peoples in the West by revealing the unsuspected complexity of the systems of thought on which their societies rest; a generosity which goes, it has to be said, with a corresponding urge to belabour Western thought for its scientistic arrogance and cult of personality. Lévi-Strauss's applications of Structuralism to such phenomena as totemism are certainly meant partly to reprove us for the centuries of mistaken belief in our own economic and technological superiority, which have led to the destruction all over the world of indigenous societies and to the plundering of the natural environment. A close connection is there for all to see between the intellectual principles which inform Structuralism and the principles of ecology, which regards the environment as a system no element of which can be considered in isolation from other, related elements. In the work of Lévi-Strauss this ecological parallel is very apparent.

He proposes his Structuralism as a way of reconciling the supposedly opposed orders of the 'etic' and the 'emic'. These two orders are also those of the empirical and the logical, or the real and the ideal. In Structuralism, if Lévi-Strauss is right, they merge, because his structures are truly intermediary between facts and theory, neither of which can be recognized as existing independently of the structure. It is Lévi-Strauss's view that this merging of the real with the logical is to be observed most readily in so-called 'primitive' societies. Thus a book like *The Savage Mind*,[12] which investigates the nature of totemism, should be read also as a *defence* of totemism, a social institution quaint to many of us but presented by Lévi-Strauss as a most resourceful, intelligent and observant ordering of the natural environment with a view to correlating the distinctions observed between species of fauna and flora with distinctions between human groups. The principle which Lévi-Strauss claims is operative in totemism is thus one of 'isomorphism', in that the structure of the surrounding human world is seen as open to correlation with that of the surrounding natural world. Lévi-Strauss is insistent that totemism is an intellectual and even an aesthetic system, not, as we might superciliously imagine, a practical one. Contrary to our received view that if indigenous peoples are conspicuously good, as they frequently are, at discriminating between plant and animal species which to us look the same, then this is because they derive practical, probably economic advantages from being so, he maintains that totemistic systems of discrimination are theoretical, because they function as models of how to make sense of the world. Totemists, in fact, are a great deal more sophisticated than they appear to be: they are practising Structuralists for whom the sensuous and intelligible are one, since the plants and animals among which they live form a differential system of meanings.

It is easy to see from such arguments as these why Lévi-Strauss has been accused of 'mentalism', a charge which he rejects on the grounds that his purpose is to move beyond the, as he sees it, facile and outmoded distinction which the Western mind insists on making between the mental and the real. Here he might be seen as following Husserl's phenomenological prescription, of keeping both subject and object in view at once, as the two poles of one axis of inquiry. The ability of the totemist to see and understand, as it were, simultaneously, is reflected by the same ability in Lévi-Strauss as a student of totemism. The difference, however, is that where the totemist is himself an idealization, Lévi-Strauss is not. The totemist is an idealization because not all totemists may be very good at totemism; some may be quite unable to recognize and apply the system of differentiation followed by their culture. This does not seem to apply to Lévi Strauss himself, despite his expressed wish to be read only as the spokesperson for Structuralism and not as the distinctive individual Claude Lévi-Strauss. If he is accepted as the mere voice of Structuralism, then he achieves the same degree of idealization for us, his readers, as the totemists whom he is writing about; but if he fails to be so accepted, and his doctrine is taken to be a personal one, his apparent modesty and self-effacement are of no avail. It is legitimate here to turn his Structuralism against him and point to the truth that to strive to achieve anonymity within a highly personalized culture such as we live in is knowingly to distinguish and thus to individualize oneself. In this respect, Lévi-Strauss's Structuralism is ambivalent.

Its effect is to endow the systems of thought which it claims to reveal with a remarkable autonomy and range. The structural models which Lévi-Strauss offers us have the same extensibility which we have already met with in the case of linguistic structures. They take account not only of the known data but also, potentially, of data yet to be discovered. They are truly theoretical in fact, in legislating for the possible as well as the actualized; and just as Chomsky's posited mental structure which we are each of us born with for language acquisition is greatly constrained by the structure of the language we actually acquire, so the Structuralist anthropologist looks on actual social structures as particular limitations of the productivity of the system. Lévi-Strauss's systems of thought, which are based on sets of binarily opposed terms and on rules of transformation by which the system is able to yield more and more actual 'events', are a reservoir of future possibilities, leaving, so far as one can see, no room for absolute innovation. Whatever forms of social organization or collective behaviour may be registered by anthropologists in the future, their possibility is already known; there is an empty pigeon-hole waiting for them in the schema drawn up on the existing evidence. These schemata are a feature of all Structuralist thought and not just of Lévi-Straussian anthropology; they point to an almost mystical belief in the sovereignty of systematic thought, which has its own rules for generating new events from a more or less stable structure.

Lévi-Strauss has thus embarked on a mighty quest, for an all-pervading and essentially timeless logic of culture and society:

> The customs of a people as a whole are always marked by a style: they form systems. I am convinced that these systems do not exist in unlimited numbers, and that human societies, like individuals – in their games, their dreams or their fantasies – never create in an absolute sense, but limit themselves to choosing certain combinations from an ideal repertoire which it would be possible to reconstitute. By drawing up an inventory of all the customs that had been observed, all those imagined in myths, those also evoked in the games of children and adults, and the dreams of healthy and sick individuals and psychopathological behaviours, one would be able to draw up a periodic table like that of the chemical elements, in which all real or merely possible customs would appear grouped in families, and in which we would simply need to recognize those which societies have in fact adopted.[13]

The breathtaking inclusiveness of this Structuralist programme, which promises to be able to incorporate within its model even the most intimate and idiosyncratic episodes of human behaviour, would not perhaps be subscribed to by many besides Lévi-Strauss himself. It is in claims of this magnitude that his Structuralism reveals itself as an ideology rather than simply a method of inquiry. But the doubts and suspicions which his extremism arouses in us should not prevent us from admiring the logic of his practical demonstrations when he settles to analyse a particular corpus of social practices or myths. The quotation I have just given opens a chapter in his autobiographical volume, *Tristes tropiques*, in which he analyses the customs, institutions, attitudes and arts of an American-Indian people called the Caduveo. There could be no better place to experience both the extraordinary ambitions of Lévi-Strauss's Structuralism and its great elegance than in this intricate but absorbing account. The analysis of Caduveo body-painting is the most arresting achievement of all perhaps, because, first, we may suppose that such an art-form can be described but not analysed and, second, because of the baffling complexity of line it seems to involve. These paintings are ideal as an object on which to demonstrate Structuralism's powers of analysis because they are seemingly both insignificant and random. Once Lévi-Strauss has attended to them they seem neither.

His analysis is built on the necessary pairs of opposed terms – men/women, carving/painting, representational-ism/abstraction, angles/curves, symmetry/asymmetry, and so on. (It is stretching things to call some of these pairs 'opposed', and an opposition such as that between rep-resentational and abstract motifs is surely one imported by the Western anthropologist, fresh from Paris.) He manages to introduce order into the bewildering multiplicity of forms in Caduveo body-painting and in so doing to accord it a dignity and seriousness not accorded to it before. He then goes on to assimilate the structure revealed in this artistic practice to the structures of Caduveo society, in a series of arguments too long and detailed to retail here. The con-clusion which Lévi-Strauss comes to, however, concerning the social function of their art is important for showing how his structural analysis can ultimately transcend the binary divisions on which it depends. Caduveo society, it seems, like any other society, is riven by what Marxists like to refer to as 'internal contradictions'. These contradictions are the consequence of their social organization and are in fact insoluble:

But the remedy that was lacking on the social plane, or which they were forbidden to envisage, could not escape them altogether. Insidiously, it helped to disturb them. And since they were unable to take cognisance of it and live it, they began to dream it. Not in a direct form which would have come up against their prejudices; in a transposed and apparently inoffensive form: in their art.[14]

And as with Caduveo art so it is with a society's myths, in the interpretation of which Lévi-Strauss has displayed an extraordinary patience and virtuosity. Myths, like art, have a function of reconciling on the imaginary plane those social contradictions which cannot be resolved on the real plane. The influence of Freud on Lévi-Strauss's thought is very apparent here, if we accept that it is Freud above all in this century who has led us to interpret mental schemata, once freed from the constraints of reality, as informed by wish-fulfilment. Both art and myth for Lévi-Strauss deal with material which societies might otherwise keep repressed; they are thus therapeutic, and may be seen as standing in a dialectical relationship to the social, economic and other intractable realities of the populations whose art and myths they are. 'Such speculations . . . do not seek to depict what is real but to justify the shortcomings of reality.'[15]

Lévi-Strauss was not the first anthropologist to grasp the high significance of myths as evidence of a society's way of understanding the world around it, but it is fair to claim that as a result of his extensive publications on the myths, chiefly, of American-Indian peoples, we now take a much less patronizing view of myth in general. Lévi-Strauss uses them to provide copious further evidence for his Structuralism. They are an ideal subject for him:

Mythology confronts the student with a situation which at first sight appears contradictory. On the one hand it would seem that in the course of a myth anything is likely to happen. There is no logic, no continuity. Any characteristic can be attributed to any subject; every conceivable relation can be found. With myth, everything becomes possible. But on the other hand, this apparent arbitrariness is belied by the astounding similarity between myths collected in widely different regions. Therefore the problem: if the content of a myth is contingent, how are we going to explain the fact that myths throughout the world are so similar?[16]

This apparent contradiction between variety and same-ness is to the Structuralist a most encouraging clue because it points to an underlying structure common to myths everywhere: and that is the structure Lévi-Strauss believes he has revealed in his analyses of myths. The technique he adopts is relatively simple, being to divide each myth up into its constituent elements or 'mythemes', to classify these 'mythemes' in terms of their 'function' within the myth and finally to relate the various classes of function to one another in an overall explanation of the structure of the myth. Lévi-Strauss is very fond of finding analogies for his procedures in those of musical composition, and he likens the effect of his analysis of myths to presenting them in the form of a musical score, where we not only read sequentially along the lines, from left to right, but also vertically from staff to staff in order to grasp the simultaneous harmonies of the music (the analogy between musical harmony and the imaginary social or cosmological 'harmony' aspired to in myth is very much part of Lévi-Strauss's argument). I shall not dwell on his actual method of analysis, because it will be more useful to do that in Chapter 4, in connection with the literary applications of Structuralism; myths being narratives the method used to analyse them may readily be extended to the fictional or other narratives our own culture is accustomed to. What Lévi-Strauss supplies is an extremely systematic reading of what had before seemed a more or less arbitrary, even chaotic story. Once again, he endows with logic what to a contemporary Western mind appears almost offensively to lack it. The analysis has its own beauty, which is the beauty of economy, since the logical explanation which Lévi-Strauss works towards serves to explain and to unify a great many data. The various levels on which those data belong are themselves ultimately shown to share a logic, as in his hugely elaborate analysis of the 'Story of Asdiwal', in which the geographi-cal, economic, sociological and cosmological aspects of a North-west American-Indian myth are made to cohere quite remarkably.[17]

· The analyst is enabled to pass from one aspect or level of the myth to others by his presumption that the patterns he discovers in the different spheres are transformations of each other. No one pattern is the master from which the others are taken as derivative; the analyst can start anywhere and hope to produce the same result. Lévi-Strauss stresses that the myth which serves as his 'reference' or starting-point in his four large and exhaustive volumes of analysis of American-Indian myths was arbitrarily chosen. There is for him no 'centre' to the great corpus of stories he is engaged on analysing and ordering.

This transformational principle is one of great importance for any Structuralism because it lays down that one surface structure be understood as a version of another. With Lévi-Strauss it operates not only within particular myths, revealing one set of relations to be a logical transformation of another set, but also between myths, revealing one myth to be the logical transformation of another, itself perhaps borrowed from a neighbouring people. In this way the autonomy of the system of mythical thought is guaranteed, since the myths themselves generate other myths, and all that human societies can claim to be is the locus of the transformations. For Lévi-Strauss the history of human culture is one of the gradual realization of more and more of the logical possibilities inherent in the Great System.

Although myths are stories they are not so obviously diachronic in their structure as the stories we are accustomed to in our own society; they do not give us when we read them the same sense of chronology or logical consequence of one episode from another. And even this weakened sense of chronology comes under attack in an analysis such as that conducted by Lévi-Strauss, which groups together related 'mythemes' taken from different parts of the story. There is still a progression in the myth, from the recognition of a conflict or contradiction to its imaginary resolution, but between these two terms of the transformation chronology plays little or no part. Music and myths, Lévi-Strauss declares, are 'machines for suppressing time',[18] even though both, of course, have to unfold in real time, which is the time of their performance. Myths are thus an excellent bridge between social anthropology and the related discipline of historiography, into which Structuralism has also moved, and to powerful effect.

This should seem wrong, since if ever there was a study committed to the rejection of the synchronic viewpoint it is surely history. Where social anthropology could hardly not have succumbed to Structuralism, given its concern for the static and the constant, history, one might think, could hardly not have stood out against it, since historians are supposedly concerned with the sequential and the changing. Anthropology and history indeed were long looked on as opposites, and the true anthropologist was urged, for example, by Radcliffe-Brown to do without what was slightingly described as 'conjectural history',[19] or those accounts offered by native informants of how the present state of things in their society had come about. Myths, too, are 'just-so' stories, purporting to explain existing states of affairs in genetic terms, which makes Lévi-Strauss's treatment of them in exclusively synchronic terms the more subversive of their apparent function.

What goes for 'conjectural history' might also seem to go for authenticated history, in those societies possessing documentary evidence of their own past. An extreme Structuralism might claim that history, or the diachronic axis of our existence in society, is irrelevant when it comes to accounting for the current state of things; and this indeed is the supposition sometimes made about Structuralism, that it is blind to the past. But this is not so. The opposition between the synchronic and diachronic points of view has been overdone. Saussure himself was never closed to the possibilities of genetic or historical explanation in questions of language, for no linguist can be. Languages change through time and they have a history which it is possible, at least in part, to re-create, partly from written

records and partly by deduction, by retrospective application of synchronic principles. Saussure was merely insistent that the synchronic and diachronic viewpoints should
not be confused, as they frequently are by amateurs of
language – the commonest example of such confusion is
the attempt to define the 'value' of a current term in the
language by reference to its etymology, as if its 'value'
today were to be determined by its value far in the past
rather than by the relations it has with other current terms.
Structuralism and historiography are not irreconcilable,
but, indeed, capable of the most fruitful collaboration.

The clear recognition by historians of the distinction
between the synchronic and diachronic axes has certain
radical consequences for the way they do history. In
relation, first, to their own position as practising historians
here and now, they may come to share Lévi-Strauss's
realization that 'History is never history . . . but history-*for*
. . .',[20] by which he means that there can be no such thing
as history-in-itself, independent of the historians who write
it, but only history-for this historian or that, who will bring
to the business of writing history a great many interests,
biases, rhetorical devices and so on that belong absolutely
to the present. Orwellian nightmares about the 'rewriting'
of the past practised by totalitarian societies should not
stop us recognizing that all societies rewrite the past as
their own needs and knowledge change. History is never
timeless but necessarily partial, a text which, because it
has been written in one age, may always be rewritten by
another. The great works of historiography which survive
their own age themselves become historical documents,
informing us richly about the age in which they were
written and its prevailing ideologies – there is a great deal
of the English eighteenth century in Gibbon, let us say, as
well as a great deal about the Roman empire, because that
mighty history was also a history-*for* the audience which
Gibbon had in view and with which he shared a culture.

As English-speakers, we may lose sight of the distinction
between history as what has been recorded of or written

about the past and the past itself, taken as what actually occurred, because the word 'history' generally covers both. It is a signifier with two crucially distinct signifieds. For present purposes, I shall prefer the term 'historiography' to history, in order to keep in mind that it is the writing of history that we are concerned with. It is easier to accept that historiography must be *for* someone because it has clearly been produced *by* someone. Historiography is a bringing of the past into the present, or at least those elements and aspects of the past in which the present takes some interest and which it may well believe have been seriously neglected.

What Lévi-Strauss challenges is what he believes to be a prejudice working in favour of diachrony and against synchrony: a form of historicism in fact, bound up with the notion of Progress and the superiority of the present in the West over any past anywhere. His Structuralism may thus be put forward as a corrective: 'The ethnologist respects history, but does not accord it a privileged value. He conceives it as a form of research complementary to his own: one opens the fan of human societies in time, the other in space.'[21] But in Structuralism, as we have seen, time can become space and space time, in the homogeneous space-time of the Structuralist's own text. The prejudice among traditional historians against synchronism stems mostly, one might argue, from the vested interest historiography has long had in causation. If historians present the past in terms of sequences, these are not random and discontinuous sequences but ones in which particular elements are shown as the causes of others coming after them. The motto under which much traditional history-writing operates is that of *Post hoc ergo propter hoc*, or 'After which therefore because of which'. Causation makes sense of the past very satisfactorily for us, and is not to be dissociated from chronology. Structuralism is suspicious of causation not because it is foolish enough to deny its efficacy but because of the misleading way in which it categorizes various elements of the past into causes and effects. The relations which Structuralism seeks to identify are two-way and a properly Structuralist way of seeing causes and effects is as the two terms of a relation. We all agree that there can be no effect without a previous cause, but find it harder to grasp that there can be no cause without a subsequent effect, for the good reason that until the effect is present the cause has not acquired its causal status. Thus causes occur not in history but in historiography, as a structural relation within the historian's text. By distributing causes and effects the historian also distributes meaning in history and historical meaning is an abstraction locatable in the last resort only in the mind of the student or reader of historiography. We should accept with A. J. Greimas that:

> Thus, any grasping of meaning has the effect of turning histories into permanences: whether we have to deal with an investigation into the meaning of a life or the meaning of a story (or of history), the investigation – the fact, that is, that we place ourselves before a linguistic manifestation in the attitude of the addressee of the message – has as its consequence that the algorithms of history present themselves as states, or in other words as static structures.[22]

Causation is a prime example of historical hindsight, and hindsight is that future-oriented interpretation of a moment in the past against which even traditional historians constantly warn one another but which they continue to practise because if they lacked hindsight there could be no historiography at all. Hindsight represents the intrusion of the historian into the field of his study bearing knowledge denied to the contemporary actors in whom he is interested. It is one of the benefits of Structuralism to have made us more acutely aware of how hindsight infects historiography and to suggest ways in which it may be partially offset.

In general, this can be done by paying less attention to chronology and less attention to the singular and exceptional deeds of individuals. The style of historiography to which Structuralism is opposed is widely known by its French name of '*l'histoire événementielle*' or 'event-history'. 'Event-history' is essentially the past atomized into the resounding exploits of Great Men and Great Institutions; of armies and their generals, and nations and their kings and political eminences. It is history written, as it were, exclusively in headlines and much taken up with the calendar or with the dating of its events. In 'event-history' the singularized moments and persons do not so much stand out against their historical context as subsume it, by coming to represent in themselves an entire society over many years.

Structuralist historiography is the exact antithesis of this. Against the old and still prevalent opinion that 'men make history' it sets the contrary opinion, that 'history makes men'. Where historians may have looked in the past mainly for 'events', the Structuralist looks for the system within which those events happened and by reference to which their historical value may be assessed.

Structuralist historiography counters the urge to singularize which is the mark of 'event-history' and which a Structuralist rejects as a sorry falsification of the past, downgrading as it does all the complex forms of knowledge, customs, beliefs and institutions which order the lives of even the most pre-eminent individuals and which also largely determine the evolution of societies. The Structuralist historian will investigate what Fernand Braudel calls 'social realities':

> By this I mean all the broad forms of collective life, economies, institutions, social architecture, civilisations in fact, above all civilisations – all of them realities of which the historians of yesterday were not ignorant, it is true, but which, except for a few astonishing precursors, they too often saw as a backcloth, arranged solely in order to explain, or as if they wanted to explain the actions of exceptional individuals on which the historian dwells so pleasurably.[23]

Braudel himself was perhaps the most distinguished recent historian willing to declare himself a Structuralist, but he did not invent Structuralist historiography, which had already been prepared for in France between the two world wars by the work of the so-called *Annales* school, centred round the historical journal of that name. Over the years the historians of *Annales*, together with their successors and imitators, have changed the course of Western historiography, away from a preoccupation with the famous – kings, emperors, commanders, prime ministers, scientific or artistic geniuses and the like – and with the more melodramatic historical events, and towards the anonymous, the unchanging, the humdrum. In the process historiography has moved closer to social anthropology, and historians have come to see that it is possible to study a given society or human group at a given moment in the past as a community of the coexistent, that historiography in short need not be afraid of taking the synchronic view. It cannot arrest time but it can take much greater account of the 'horizontal' dimension within time. Structuralism has inspired a widespread move away from the agitated tempo characteristic of 'event-history', in which dramatic events and picturesque individuals follow one another all too loudly across the stage, to the exclusion of those years and classes of society too uneventful or humble to meet its criteria of what is actually 'historical'. Structuralist historiography slows things down, by attempting to reconstruct the permanent or more or less permanent constraints within which all these events occurred, and also broadens things out, by concerning itself with the whole of contemporary societies instead of just with those elements of it fortunate enough to have singled themselves out. It takes a deliberate interest in the *uneventful*, because so very large a part of all lives, past or present, is uneventful. Exceptional persons and events can only be fully understood as such once we know what they were the exceptions from. Structuralism may reasonably claim to shift historiography in the direction of a greater realism. It prefers the study of homogeneous groups of people to that of Great Men, being drawn thereby to the statistical assessment of the past

rather than the biographical. A biographical style of historiography, devoted to tracing the careers of the few, has a
foreshortening effect on the past because of the way in
which narrative urges us ever onwards towards, in the case
of biography, the eclipse or more likely the death of its
subject. Such an approach is inescapably tied to an ideology
of change, of the 'short run'. Structuralist historiography,
on the other hand, is famous for its obsession with the
'long run', a perspective which is dominated, 'for good or
ill', remarks Braudel, by the term 'structure':

> By *structure*, observers of the social understand an organisation,
> a coherence, fairly fixed relations between realities and social
> masses. For we historians a structure is no doubt an assem-
> blage, an architecture, but even more a reality which time
> wears away only slowly and transmits over long periods.
> Certain long-lived structures become stable elements for infinite
> generations: they encumber their history and hinder – that is,
> govern – its development. Others are quicker to crumble away.
> But all are both supports and obstacles.[24]

The title of Braudel's own major work of historiography,
The Mediterranean in the Reign of Philip II, is an excellent
indication of the profound shift which his structure-mind-
edness leads to. It is provocative to take a geographical
unit such as the Mediterranean as the focus of a work
dealing with a period of European history full traditionally
of the exploits of the rulers of empires and nation-states. But
when it comes to the *longue durée*, or long run, geographical
structures are clearly those which last longest of all and
which may well exert the severest as well as the most
formative constraints on the history of a population. A
perspective such as Braudel's gives a higher priority to the
continuities of life imposed by climate and topography, as
well as to those human activities – agriculture, industry,
commerce – most immediately dependent on them. In thus
integrating historiography with geography, geology and
economics, the Structuralist mode of historiography bears
out the promise that Structuralism works to unify knowledge. In an extreme form it may even claim to be able to

deliver a 'total history', which would be to construct a sort of working model of some particular group or society at a particular moment of its history, of the same density and complexity as we are aware of as members of our own group or society here and now. Few would accept that such completeness is even hypothetically attainable, if only because of the inevitable admixture of the historian's own 'mentality' with that which he is seeking from his data to reconstruct.

In principle, a historian who pursues a Structuralist method should be less likely to impose his own preconceptions on his evidence, taking it as his task to render that evidence coherent without anachronism. The many attempts now being made by historians to depict the 'mentality' of a particular group or class of people in the past are of this kind. Such a 'mentality' is not psychological, in the sense that it is not to be supposed to have been found within the mind of this or that individual within the group or class in question. It is the historian's construct and thus an idealization, a hypothetical 'group-mind' recreated in order to explain various social or cultural 'events' in a particular period.

Historiography of this sort is both humane and tending towards if never quite attaining objectivity. The historian's own role is to assemble and arrange data rather than explicitly to interpret them. In the words of a French historian of ideas popularly associated with Structuralism, and constantly anxious to keep his distance from any such label, the historian is an 'archaeologist' and his job is to give an 'intrinsic description of the monument'.[25] The monument, however, is not the past as such but what remains of the past in the present by way of archival materials of every kind. The characteristic of these materials on which Foucault concentrates is their discontinuity; our records of the past are worse than incomplete, they are a paltry survival of cultures, civilizations and historical epochs of infinite complexity. Narrative historiography, of the kind most of us grew up with, is particularly clever at hiding from us the sorry gaps and discontinuities in the evidence on which it is based; it hides them, wittingly or not, by the continuities of its own prose and the use of imagination. Thus a contemporary historian who is faced with supplying the motive for some historical action will supply it from his own psychological knowledge, probably on the assumption that psychological knowledge is scientific and so valid for all periods and places. A Structuralist would argue that this assumption is wrong, and that the psychology of an age must be learned, if possible, from the surviving documents of that age: human motives are not timeless but culture-bound. To explain the actions of an Elizabethan adventurer by 'ambition', let us suppose, is not the same as explaining the actions of a Victorian entrepreneur by a similar trait; the role and nature of 'ambition' in the two ages may be quite different. Ambition, too, has a history.

Structuralism has the advantage here that its explanatory models always *display* their essential discontinuity, in contrast to the continuities of life itself. It is one of the paradoxes of chronology that it should impress us as embodying the continuity of experience when in fact it signals the very opposite. A chronology is by definition a *broken* record which persuades us without much difficulty to overlook the breaks. Traditional historiography tricks us into accepting that the temporal series in which it arranges historical events are those pertaining to the events themselves rather than to the historian's own culture. The time-scales or temporal 'codes' used by historians are not even congruent with one another, as Lévi-Strauss takes pleasure in observing, pointing out that the time-scale used, say, by a prehistorian, in which there may be millions of years between 'events', would, if applied to a modern society, have the effect of abolishing almost everything that had ever happened in it. His conclusion is that: 'If the general code does not consist of dates which can be arranged in linear series, but in classes of dates each of which provides its own autonomous system of reference, the discontinuous and classificatory nature of historical knowledge appears clearly.'[26]

Lévi-Strauss delights in thus drawing the attention of the historical profession to the fact many of them may be reluctant to admit, that their temporal series are so many 'codes'. The advantage which the Structuralist may claim is not that he is exempt from operating within a particular, arbitrary temporal 'code' but that he is conscious of doing so. He accepts the relativism of what he is doing. Where traditional historiography sought to hide the gaps in the accounts it presented of the past, the Structuralist historian may, as Foucault recommends, bring them to the fore: 'Discontinuity was the stigma of temporal dispersal which it was the historian's job to suppress from history. It has now become one of the fundamental elements of historical analysis.'[27]

Foucault's objections to being called a Structuralist historian seem to follow largely from his wish to present historiography as an autonomous discipline, which had already adopted Structuralist methods without being prompted from outside. It had done so because of the ever-increasing importance which historians accorded to economic factors in history, partly under the influence of Marxism, with its insistence that in any society economic relations, or the relations of production, are primary and that everything else – the 'superstructure' of ideas, customs, beliefs – can eventually be explained as deriving from them. Economics, be it noted, is the structural study *par excellence*, as Saussure himself recognized by citing it as a model for his own synchronic linguistics. An economy is the ideal example of a functioning whole all of whose parts interact and depend utterly on one another. It has a history and historical explanations may be offered for particular features of its current condition; but the proper *economic* explanation of that condition is synchronic, to be determined by observation of the various very complex relations which constitute the economy. Increasingly, such observation is achieved nowadays by constructing computer 'models' of the economy, which is unadulterated Structuralism. The noted failure of such model-building to produce useful practical consequences, as opposed to theoretical insights, need not be held against the Structuralist method. But the Saussurean concept of linguistic 'value', of which I have already made so much, is basically an economic one; and the fact that our present generation is more keenly aware than most of how economic values fluctuate for structural reasons helps to bring out the great significance of Saussure's metaphor.

At the time of his death Foucault held the perhaps strange-sounding appointment of Professor of the History of Systems of Thought at the Collège de France in Paris. The title was created to suit the man, in recognition of the kind of historiography he had so conspicuously practised. In his best-known book, *The Order of Things*, Foucault had introduced the notion of the 'épistème' as a way of characterizing particular historical periods according to the manner in which they made sense of the world around them. (*Epistème* is the Greek word for 'knowledge' and familiar to us as a part of the longer term 'epistemology', which is that branch of philosophy that concerns itself with the theory of knowledge.) The claim which Foucault advances is that each age organizes its knowledge differently from preceding and succeeding ages, but that within the circumference of a particular *épistème* different branches of knowledge will organize their data according to the same principles. Foucault assimilates data from three, as one might think, disparate sciences – language, economics and natural history – to try and prove that all share a common system of ordering. Synchronicity is all-powerful:

> If the natural history of Tournefort, Linnaeus and Buffon relates to anything other than itself, it is not to biology, to the comparative anatomy of Cuvier or the evolutionism of Darwin, it is to the general grammar of Bauzée, to the analysis of money and wealth such as one finds in Law, Veron de Fortbonnais or Turgot.[28]

That is, by their contemporaries shall ye know them, and not by their predecessors or their successors. If Foucault's method were generally followed it would have the effect of introducing all manner of discontinuities into the smooth flow of historiography. A conventional historian of biological ideas would not be happy to evaluate eighteenth-century biology by relating it to eighteenth-century linguistics or political economy, of which he will most likely know nothing; he would rather relate it to the biology that came before and after. In so doing he falls back into the teleological historiography to which Structuralism is opposed, whereby the ideas of one period are understood either as an improvement on those of earlier periods or as a mere preparation for the better ideas that succeeded them, as if the minds of biologists and others were bent always on the future and not on the present. The force of Foucault's *épistème*, which results in the apparent severance of one historical period from another, is considerable, and Foucault seems carefully to have avoided ever suggesting how historiography might best pass from period to period without reinstating the old illusion of continuity.

Foucault is an extreme sceptic: he does not propose that his kind of historiography will reach closer to the actuality of the past. Rather the reverse: he is at all times categorical in his insistence that what he has to work with as a historian are the surviving documents which, because they are 'textual', can never be direct or immediate evidence of how things were in the past but only mediate and therefore also 'rhetorical' evidence of how contemporaries recorded and understood their own times. The material with which this ultra-self-conscious historiography has to work is thus what Foucault terms the 'discursive formations' it is able to identify in the data available to it. These form a kind of categorical grid which each age places over reality in order to comprehend it: 'that designation of the visible which, by a sort of prelinguistic sorting, enables it to be transcribed in language.'[29] These 'discursive formations' do not have the unity which other Structuralist historians would claim to have located in their 'mentalities'. Foucault criticizes the idea of a discoverable or re-creatable 'mentality' as the mark of a given age or social group for this very reason, that it imposes a centralized conception of a historical period which then becomes an agency by which to explain a whole variety of contemporary phenomena, even though those phenomena were originally the data from which the characteristics of the 'mentality' were deduced. Rather than succumb to that circular procedure, Foucault insists on the limitations of his data and on the incompatibilities that may be observed between them equally with the convergences. He is a post-Structuralist in his adherence to the principle of dispersion as against the principle of unification. Moreover, as a historian he emphasizes passionately the mechanisms that have existed in all historical ages for *controlling* discourse: that is, for permitting certain facts, opinions and ideas to be uttered while forbidding others. All discourse, according to Foucault, is subject to the power of those in authority, so that the discursive structures that he may uncover as a historian need to be seen as authoritarian and repressive. As a libertarian he looks on historiography, together with the documents it rests on, as a conspiracy of the powerful and orthodox againt the powerless and eccentric.

This suspicion has nothing to do with Structuralism, which is far from containing Foucault even if his ideas about historiography converge at many points with Structuralist views. Structuralism, as practised by Braudel, believes that historiography can accede to certain truths about the past, and that a Structuralist historiography can accede to them more closely than other kinds. Foucault is too much of a Nietzschean to allow any such simple belief. Discourse is discourse, so far as he is concerned, and the 'true' discourse no different from any other, being a certain rhetorical strategy that aims to extend the power or authority of one social group over another. Truth as a concept is not exempt from the power-game or the game of 'desire' that Foucault sees as being played simultaneously with it.

'True discourse' is vitiated because 'it cannot recognise the will to truth that traverses it.'[30] Such declarations lend force to his complaint that those who label him as a Structuralist only draw attention to a gap in their own vocabulary. He will not be coerced by their discourse or become the victim of their unacknowledged will to power over him!

NOTES

1. N. Troubetskoy, *Psychologie du langage*, pp. 245–6.
2. L. Althusser, *Pour Marx*, p. 17.
3. J. Derrida, *Edmund Husserl's 'Origin of Geometry': An Introduction*, p. 161.
4. E. Husserl, *Shorter Works*, ed. P. McCormick and F. A. Elliston, p. 25.
5. W. Köhler, *Gestalt Psychology*, p. 62.
6. *Ibid.*, p. 39.
7. A. Radcliffe-Brown, *Structure and Function in Primitive Society*, p. 190.
8. E. Gellner, *Relativism and the Social Sciences*, p. 136.
9. C. Lévi-Strauss, Introduction to Jakobson, *Six Lectures on Sound and Meaning*, p. xii.
10. Lévi-Strauss, *Structural Anthropology*, p. 34.
11. Lévi-Strauss, *The View from Afar*, p. 116.
12. 'The Savage Mind' is a misleading translation of the original title, *La Pensée sauvage*, because it fails altogether to convey the meaning of 'unofficial' present in the French term *sauvage* (the French for a 'wildcat strike', e.g., is *une grève sauvage*'). 'Untamed' is a suggestion which has been put forward as the best English translation of 'sauvage' as Lévi-Strauss is using it. 'The Savage Mind' is especially unfortunate for reinforcing the very tendency Lévi-Strauss is so set on removing from Western minds: that which sees 'primitive' peoples as inferior and uncivilized.
13. Lévi-Strauss, *Tristes tropiques*, p. 153.
14. *Ibid.*, p. 169.
15. Lévi-Strauss, *Anthropologie structurale Tome 2*, p. 30.
16. Lévi-Strauss, *Structural Anthropology*, p. 208.
17. An excellent English translation of this analysis can be found in *The Structural Study of Myth and Totemism*, ed. E. Leach.
18. Lévi-Strauss, *Mythologiques Tome 1*, p. 23.
19. Radcliffe-Brown, op. cit., p. 50.
20. Lévi-Strauss, *La Pensée sauvage*, p. 341.

21. *Ibid.*, p. 339.
22. A. J. Greimas, *Du sens*, p. 104.
23. F. Braudel, *Ecrits sur l'histoire*, p. 23.
24. *Ibid.*, p. 50.
25. M. Foucault, *L'Archéologie du savoir*, p. 15.
26. Lévi-Strauss, *La Pensée sauvage*, p. 345.
27. Foucault, op. cit., p. 16.
28. Foucault, *Les Mots et les choses*, p. 14.
29. *Ibid.*, p. 150.
30. Foucault, *L'Ordre du discours*, p. 22.

3
SEMIOTICS

The Structuralism employed in anthropology by Lévi-Strauss and others derives directly from the Structuralism practised in linguistics; Lévi-Strauss has declared his allegiance to the insights of Saussure and of Jakobson, even if he has at times pressed the analogy between his methods and theirs too hard, in proposing, for example, that marriage-rules and kinship systems be seen as a language which allows of the circulation of women just as spoken or written language allows of the circulation of words. This analogy has been keenly criticized as misleading, and one might conclude that Lévi-Straussian Structuralism is at best a loose and at worst a metaphorical derivative of the Saussurean model, though an invigorating and absorbing method of research in its own right.[1]

The Structuralism of contemporary historians acknowledges little or no debt to linguistic Structuralism. As we have seen in the case of Foucault, historians prefer to attribute the undoubted success of structural methods in historiography to an indigenous development within the discipline, founded largely on its new reliance on economic, demographic and other 'structural' data. As a consequence, it is most uncommon for historians to declare themselves to be Structuralists, when it is enough for them to reveal their affiliations by some other description; anyone these days calling him- or herself a 'social historian' is likely to pursue a method of research broadly conforming with Structuralism.

In the rest of this volume, however, I shall be dealing with direct and explicit projections of Structuralist ideas and methods outside the narrowly linguistic sphere. The first of these projections is into what is called, variously, Semiotics or Semiology, terms deriving, as I have earlier indicated, from the Greek word for 'sign': *semeion*. Semiotics or semiology is quite simply the study of signs or of systems of signs and represents the largest possible extension of Structuralist ideas into the investigation of human culture. In principle, it is more embracing than social anthropology, which has traditionally restricted itself to particular social and cultural institutions, rather than attempt to study culture as a whole. Semiotics/semiology knows no such limitation.

First, though, there is the matter of the two terms themselves, Semiotics and Semiology. Assuming, as I shall do at this point of the argument, that they both name precisely the same science or study, they can be said to be two terms with a common referent. As Saussure would put it, their 'signification' is the same. This does not make them identical, however, because they refer to their common referent in distinct ways. They have different 'values'. They form, in fact, a pair of terms just like the one adduced by the German logician Frege to draw his influential distinction between the 'referent' of a term and its 'sense'; Frege's example being the terms 'morning star' and 'evening star', both of which may be used to refer to the same astral body. The two alternative terms constitute two distinct 'senses' or *forms* of reference. It is not hard to see that we may think about a particular star differently according to whether we hear it named 'morning star' or 'evening star'; the implications or connotations of the two expressions will not be the same. The choice of one over the other may well be determined by the time of day rather than by some emotive purpose on the part of the user. But this still does not make the two expressions equivalent. Indeed, given the strong contrast between the variable elements of the two expressions, 'morning' and 'evening', a Structuralist might claim them as a pair in binary opposition one with the other, so that the one *implies* the other (though the opposition and hence the implication is weaker between 'morning' and 'evening' than it is between the true opposition, 'night' and 'day').

This distinction between the 'senses' of terms or expressions which are not the same but which can be used to refer to the same object is one I have touched on in the discussion of structural linguistics. It is of great importance for the study of signs, which makes it happily appropriate that this study, as a referent, should be referrable to by two different expressions. The distinction between Semiotics and Semiology, as alternatives, requires interpretation by the very methods which Semiotics and Semiology themselves bring to the interpretation of all signs, linguistic or otherwise.

Briefly, the two terms are distinct for historical and geographical reasons. Semiotics is a term with a much longer and nobler history than Semiology. Its use can be traced back to the ancient Greeks, and it recurs in the work of the English philosopher John Locke in the late seventeenth century before having a considerable revival in this century in North America. Semiology is more of a parvenu; it was the obscure term taken over and used by Saussure himself to refer to the study of sign-systems, and, unlike its rival, it has not travelled outside Western Europe. Thus, the connotations of the two terms vary considerably. Someone declaring themselves to be a semiotician is declaring an affiliation with the North American tradition of sign-study, whereas the person who presents him- or herself as a semiologist is declaring an affiliation with the tradition descending from Saussure. The two terms thus themselves form an opposition, of different connotations. There are differences of emphasis and even of method between Semiotics as it has developed in North America, and Semiology as it has developed in Europe, and these differences may be 'read' by the informed reader into the difference between the descriptive labels themselves. Such a process of interpretation, the methods for conducting which form the essential interest of the semiotician or semiologist, may itself be called *semiosis*.

From now on I shall stick to the term Semiotics to refer to the study of signs, though there will be occasion to revert later on to the distinctions in 'value' between this term and its rival, Semiology. Semiotics, clearly, is akin to certain branches of philosophy, notably those which study inference. Some semioticians indeed have not wished to distinguish between Semiotics and logic, interpreted in the widest sense, since both take it as their task to codify the rules of thought. Thus the history of Semiotics is intimately bound up with the history of philosophy. But it is not *only* bound up with the history of philosophy, because Semiotics has far wider implications, certainly, than logic lays claim to. Compared with logic it is highly pragmatic, because the inferences with which it is concerned are ones which pervade our everyday lives. They are the inferences by which we make sense, or fail to make sense, of our environment. Semiotics is profoundly social, because of the fundamental role which signs play in every moment of human life and of our interaction in society.

As a preliminary example of the pervasiveness of signs in our lives, and hence of the potential ubiquity of Semiotics, I will take those bodily signs which doctors, and patients, know more familiarly by the name of symptoms. It is an interesting fact that for centuries before the term Semiology came back into currency as a consequence of its use by Saussure, the nearly identical term 'semeiology' had been in service in the medical profession in England to refer to that branch of medicine which studies symptoms. (The redundant-seeming second *e* in 'semeiology' we can safely say connotes 'greekness', being directly traceable to the Greek term *semeion*; and the study of symptoms began with the Greeks, so far as our own medical tradition is concerned.) Symptoms are signs of some bodily malfunction. They lead whoever knows the correct way to interpret them to the name and hence the nature of the disorder they are the symptoms of. The interpretation of the doctor is thus an inference, and the symptom or sign something which is not itself the illness but which leads a properly trained physician *to* the illness. In the medical context signs are the visible or otherwise sensible representatives of what would otherwise remain undetected, the archetypal medical symptom being a mark of some sort on the surface of the afflicted body which must be read as evidence of some trouble within the body, or of trouble of a kind more generalized than would be apparent to a wholly ignorant layman from the localized symptom.[2] The interpretation of the symptom by the doctor is, as I have said, an inference, but it is also, one must appreciate, a *conventional* inference, made in terms of the medical knowledge actually or potentially available to that doctor in that society at that time. That is, the doctor must know *how* to interpret the symptom, and it is this insertion of the medical datum into a prevailing system of cultural knowledge which also marks its insertion into the field of semiotics: 'The first doctor who discovered a constant relation between a series of red spots on the face and measles, drew an inference; but once this relation had become a conventional one, and been recorded in medical treatises, then we got a SEMIOTIC CONVENTION'[3] (Eco's capitals).

As signs, then, symptoms have the property of leading the mind of their medical interpreter on, causing it to pass from what is before it to what is not before it. Nothing can be a sign or a symptom *in itself*. Red spots on the face of someone feeling unwell are a symptom only for those with the small amount of medical knowledge or powers of interpretation required to read them as such. One might say that they become a symptom only with their interpretation, in just the same way as the cause of an effect becomes so only once the effect is in place. A sign, in the definition of another seventeenth-century English philosopher, Thomas Hobbes (given the neglect into which Semiotics fell in this country after Hobbes and Locke, and in which it has remained even in the recent years of its revival elsewhere, the seventeenth century has to go down as its English heyday):

> ... is the evident antecedent of the consequent; and contrarily, the consequent of the antecedent, when the like consequences have been observed before: and the oftener they have been observed, the less uncertain is the sign. And therefore he that has most experience in any kind of business, has most signs, whereby to guess at the future time; and consequently is the most prudent: and so much more prudent than he that is new in that kind of business, as not to be equalled by any advantage of natural and extemporary wit: though perhaps many young men think the contrary.[4]

Prudence is a virtue on which Hobbes sets an unexpectedly high value, as the means to a long and secure life, but it is not incumbent on all those semiotically inclined. In this passage, however, Hobbes introduces a connection between semiotic capacity and sound citizenship which can be found strenuously developed in the work of some modern semioticians – differently yet also convergently, in the American Charles Morris and the Frenchman Roland Barthes. It is part of the claim of Semiotics that the more competent we are at the reading of the infinitely many signs around us in daily life, the more alertly and intelligently we will live. I will come back to this claim.

Medical symptoms have the advantage, as examples of the class of signs, of not being in themselves linguistic. They serve to widen the context of thought about signs as it needs to be widened when one passes from language to communication in general. This is not to hide that medical symptoms will in nearly every case of their occurrence be interpreted in words: the patient's red spots will lead the doctor to the word 'measles' – that is, to a linguistic sign. It may also happen that the doctor will not think it worth naming the patient's complaint but will reach straight into his bag and produce some tablets. This piece of medical behaviour would be treated by some if not all semioticians as an act of interpretation, depending as it does on recognition of the particular symptoms. There is no knowing whether the word 'measles' has entered the doctor's consciousness in between whiles, or whether he is able to prescribe treatment without any such resort to the signs of language. If his response is 'purely' habitual, or 'mindless' in terms of behaviourism, that does not prevent it being construed as interpretive. No hard and fast distinction need be made, from the semiotic point of view, between the interpretation of a sign by the use of other signs, or words, and its interpretation by resort to direct action. Semiotically speaking, words are actions and actions words: and both, in context, are signs.

The pre-eminence of language among the many systems of signs available to us in society is not to be doubted, for ultimately it is hard to think of a system of non-verbal signs whose signs can go on being usefully exchanged without at some point being translated into language. As practised drivers we move our cars forward without conscious thought when a traffic signal changes from red to green; but there was almost certainly a time, before we were drivers, when the significance of this change of colour had to be explained to us in words. Without the text of the 'Highway Code' traffic signals would be meaningless for anyone strange to them. The pre-eminence of language among sign-systems was famously brought out indeed by Locke when he declared 'articulate sounds' to be the 'most convenient' and therefore the most generally used signs whereby people communicate their thoughts.[5] But this pre-eminence does not mean that the field of Semiotics is coextensive with that of Saussurean linguistics. It is both wider and narrower: wider because it takes in other than verbal signs, and narrower because the semiotic function of language is only one aspect of it.

Saussure himself, in his brief but canonical formulation of Semiology in the *Course in General Linguistics*, recognizes the pre-eminence of language but also that to study signs is to study something more than language:

A language is a system of signs expressing ideas, and hence comparable to writing, the deaf-and-dumb alphabet, symbolic

76

rites, forms of politeness, military signals, and so on. It is simply the most important of such systems.

It is therefore possible to conceive of a science *which studies the role of signs as part of social life*. It would form part of social psychology, and hence of general psychology. We shall call it semiology . . . It would investigate the nature of signs and the laws governing them. Since it does not yet exist, one cannot say for certain that it will exist. But it has a right to exist, a place ready for it in advance. Linguistics is only one branch of this general science.[6] (Saussure's italics)

The first mention of the term Semiology occurs in a manuscript of Saussure's dated 1894; in the ninety years which have passed since then it cannot be said that the science whose place was ready for it has come properly into being. Neither Semiology nor its American equivalent Semiotics has made the headway it should have done, in institutional terms. There are still relatively few universities or other institutions where it is taught or pursued professionally. Given the scope and attractions of the subject this is a pity, but it may well have been held back, and continue to be so, by its sheer pervasiveness. There is no branch of study or knowledge into which semiotics cannot usefully probe, because there is no branch of study or knowledge which is not sign-based, either because it has evolved sign-systems of its own, like mathematics or formal logic, or because it is reliant upon natural language. Like Structuralism itself therefore, Semiotics may be practised unwittingly, by those who turn their attention to the systems of signs which their particular discipline or profession employs, or to the particular uses made there of our common linguistic system of signs. The lack of semioticians specifically so called does not mean that semiotic understanding or concern is not widespread. A good deal of the research done, for example, in socio-linguistics and other branches of social psychology might well come under the heading of Semiotics.

It was the view of the leading theorist of the North American semiotic school, C. S. Peirce, that 'the entire universe ... is perfused with signs, if it is not composed exclusively of signs'.[7] If this view is correct, then the semiotician's potential subject-matter knows no bounds, even if his concern is with the method or theory of signs rather than with their extent. What Peirce seems to have meant by this daunting assertion was that the universe *as we know it* is composed exclusively of signs: he is making a distinction between the universe as it really is, or may really be, independently of the mind, and the universe as known in human cognition. The cognitive universe is formed of signs because it is the universe as already turned into words. Peirce is echoing the traditional philosophical distinction between the sensible and intelligible universes (bearing in mind that the distinction itself belongs on the intelligible side of the divide, as does the notion of 'sense-data': we cannot, in language, have access to the non-intelligible). Whatever we know, then, we know as a sign, we know it to be significant and thus communicable. Semiotics has as its realm the forms of signification.

The semiotic function itself is most easily grasped perhaps by way of the terms introduced by the Danish linguist Louis Hjelmslev (a tireless introducer of new and complex terms into both linguistics and semiotics): those of *content* and *expression*, which are Hjelmslev's extended versions of Saussure's *signified* and *signifier*. The function of any sign-system, linguistic or otherwise, is to correlate the two planes of *content* and *expression* and each such correlation of the two constitutes a sign. Hjelmslev's terms for the two parties to this contract are perhaps preferable to Saussure's in that they are more familiar and more readily graspable. I shall stick to them in this chapter.

It is legitimate, and indeed helpful, to use the term 'contract' to describe the semiotic function because of the conventional nature of the correlation between the planes of content and expression. These correlations are, inescapably and in every single case, cultural and not 'natural' ones. This point is quite easily made in respect of language itself, as we briefly saw when considering Saussure's principle of the 'arbitrariness' of the verbal sign. The correlations made by one language between expression and content may or may not coincide with those made by another. We may assume that no two languages make exactly the same correlations throughout the whole range of expression: this is what Hjelmslev is getting at when he asserts that '. . . no universal formation exists, only a universal principle of formation.'[8] He is restating the founding principle of Saussure, that as a system of signs language is autonomous in respect of reality. We can use it, to take an obvious example, to say what isn't in the world, as well as what is. And since we come to know the world through whatever language we have been born into the midst of, it is legitimate to argue that our language determines reality, rather than reality our language.

At the risk of confusing matters rather than clarifying them, I shall bring in here a further distinction which Hjelmslev makes. This is between *form* and *substance*, a distinction which has to be recognized on the planes of both expression and content. On the plane of expression in human language, it is fairly simple to grasp the distinction, which is the one we have already met with in distinguishing the sounds of a language, or phonemes, from the continuum of non-linguistic sound capable of being produced by the human speech apparatus. Phonemes are forms, the continuum of undifferentiated sound is the substance. On the plane of linguistic content the distinction is a little more elusive, being between the content as actually differentiated by a language or other system of signs, and what lies beyond the content: i.e., the continuum we call the world, that inexhaustible and transcendent source from which the content itself derives. On this plane, the content as divided up by any particular language – and all, remember, will divide it up differently – is the forms, and the world 'beyond' language is the substance. This 'beyond' is the equivalent of the cloudy, undifferentiated 'thought' which Saussure posited as the substratum of our actual ideas. It is the actual astral body, for instance, which is *both* the 'morning star' and the 'evening star', according to taste. But it is also a problem, since we have experience only of the forms and not of the substance, in Hjelmslev's terms: in order to indicate the 'beyond' in the case of Frege's star, all I have been able to do is to produce a third 'form': the form 'actual astral body'. The attempt to escape from language turns out to have been made *in* language.

The importance of this further distinction of Hjelmslev's is that it enables him to specify that restricted part of the overall scheme which is of concern to him as a semiotician: which is the correlation of *forms* and this alone. The substance, be it of expression or of content, is of no immediate concern. Phonetics and semantics may be left, therefore, to others.

This is an austere limitation in one way, though proper for the scientist that Hjelmslev saw himself to be, because if strictly observed it means that semioticians may involve themselves with the syntax of their systems of signs, and their theoretical strengths and weaknesses, but be unwilling to go on from there to the actual interpretation of signs in their social uses. This is to study the grammar of signs and forget the anthropology; and if currently there are two schools of thought within Semiotics, as there seem to be, this may stem from the sense some semioticians have that the actual interpretation of cultural signs is none of their business, that their job is to stick to the formal aspects of the subject. But for those who are not professional semioticians, it is the practical side of Semiotics that is the more rewarding, since a proper grounding in the relatively few and simple rules it involves can turn anybody into a more acute and informed 'reader' of the vastly many cultural signs by which we are surrounded.

If the 'theory of communication' had not now become rather narrowly defined by engineers, as being concerned with the successful transmission of messages irrespective of their content, then one might say that Semiotics too was a theory of communication, because all signs, linguistic or other, signify by virtue of being known to more than one person. They are conventional and institutionalized, and our knowing this, in proffering them, is our guarantee that the person we proffer them to, provided they are not wholly alien to our own cultural conventions, will understand us. It is a stipulation of Semiotics that whatever does not function within a communicative system cannot be a sign: that there can be no truly 'private' signs. The semiotic answer to the celebrated question raised by Wittgenstein, of whether there can be a 'private language' – 'And sounds which no one else understands but which "I appear to understand" might be called a "private language"'[9] – is that any system that may be called a 'language' must be at least potentially a public one: others may be taught the meaning of sounds I understand myself, since the necessary correlations of sound and sense, expression and content are in place. Private or not, they are conventional.

The fact that a sign *must* be conventional in order to qualify as a sign does not mean that everyone we use signs to has to be party to the convention in question. Just as we may use the signs of our native language to other natives who do not know those particular signs and so do not understand them, so we may elaborate conventions which hold between ourselves and only one other person or even with ourselves alone. 'Secret' languages are no different in kind from language in general; they merely function as what are sometimes called 'restricted codes'.

By this stipulation, that signs be either public or able to be made public, Semiotics guards itself against being turned into a branch of individual psychology. A conventional sign remains a conventional sign irrespective of the private intentions of the person using it. One tradition in contemporary Semiotics carries this exclusion of the sign-user's motives to the limit, declaring, for example, that 'Semiotics may be defined as the study of processes of communication, that is, the means used to influence others and recognised as such by those one seeks to influence.'[10] This tradition, especially strong among the followers of the

American semiotician Charles Morris, is behaviouristic in thus limiting itself to patent and successful acts of communication, or 'semic acts' as the writer quoted above, Eric Buyssens, likes to call them. It is the prime contention of such as Buyssens that it takes two to create a 'semic act', which is surely the case, even though a successful 'semic act' may also take place in the imagination of a single individual communicating with him- or herself. But what is not so surely the case is whether it is necessary, as Buyssens and others maintain, for both parties to the act to be *similarly* aware of what is passing between them. In a great many acts of communication, they will be, but not in all. Such a narrowly based model does not take adequate account of failed 'semic acts', where the sign apparatus malfunctions and no message or a wrong message passes; nor, more crucially for Semiotics, does it take adequate account of those 'semic acts' where no explicit attempt is being made at communication at all. There are many occasions in life when we may 'communicate' without meaning to, or in ways we cannot control, and this raises most important questions for Semiotics. Another semiotic tradition, exemplified most powerfully by Roland Barthes, has always taken a wider view of the matter than the tradition represented by Buyssens, and supposed that communication may be inadvertent. A 'semic act', that is, does not necessarily entail the connivance of the two parties to it. The distinction is well brought out by a French linguist and strong opponent of Barthes, as being one between 'true communication and mere manifestation, or between communication and signification'.[11] The question hinges seemingly on the word 'true' as Mounin uses it: 'true communication' requiring an intention to communicate in one party to the 'semic act' and a corresponding presumption in the other party that he or she has understood the act *as intended*. Barthes was quite opposed to such presumptions. He argues for a much higher level of uncertainty or even downright ambiguity in the 'semic act'. The only certainty is that the constituents of the act are *signs* and therefore that they signify; what they signify is not always sure and it may require the expertise of the semiotician to try and decide the question. The distinction between the two traditions in Semiotics, of those who would limit it to acts of 'true' communication, and those who prefer to widen it to take in all acts of signification, has large implications, to be kept in mind for the rest of this chapter.

All signs form a relation between the two planes of expression and content, but not all signs form it alike. There is a need in Semiotics to classify signs according to how they relate expression to content. They may all be conventional, but they are not by any means all as 'arbitrary' as the linguistic sign. Some linguistic signs, indeed, strike us as less arbitrary than others, or even as not arbitrary at all but 'natural': so-called onomatopoeic words are assumed to be founded on a 'natural' relation between the plane of expression, or sound, and the plane of content, or sense. We assume that an English word like *whoosh* mimics the noise of which it is the linguistic expression. And the same claim is also sometimes made for exclamations – *ouch*, *wow*, *tut*, and so on – which are likewise held to be forms conditioned by their sense. But all such forms are, as Saussure was prompt to warn us, conventional and subject to exactly the same forces of change as any other sign of the language. Onomatopoeic words vary from language to language and so do exclamations of pain, surprise and so on. They would vary much less, if at all, if their form was determined exclusively by their sense. The undoubted fact that a certain degree of mimicry is apparent in the names of, for example, birds producing a distinctive cry, does not exempt the linguistic forms in question from the laws of language, nor does it make them any the less conventional.

It does alert us, however, to the need to introduce a few broad distinctions into any typology of signs according to the nature of the relation between expression and content. The typology which has found greatest favour among semioticians is that which was developed by C. S. Peirce in the later years of the last century. Peirce returned again and again to the problem of distinguishing and classifying signs and the system with which he ended up, listing as it does no fewer than sixty-six distinct kinds of sign, is a monument to his assiduity even if its complexity has rendered it nearly useless as a working model for others. Semioticians continue to work at this question and to introduce ever subtler distinctions between kinds of signs. Such is their pleasure. It is not necessary for others to recognize such subtleties; broad distinctions may be made which are sufficient for all but an expert.

Peirce divides signs into three classes: 'symbols', 'indices' and 'icons'. Symbols we have already met with because in Peirce's classification the signs of a language are symbolic.[12] For Peirce a symbol is 'a sign which refers to the object that it denotes by virtue of a law, usually an association of general ideas, which operates to cause the symbol to be interpreted as referring to that object.'[13]

Thus, with symbols the relation of expression to content is 'arbitrary': there is no 'natural' link between one and the other. The meanings of symbols have to be learned by those who employ them – there is no deducing without help or instruction the content of the expressions of a language utterly unknown to us. A point also needing to be made about Peirce's definition of a symbol is that the 'object' he speaks of must not be identified with an object in the world. This is where Hjelmslev's terminology comes into its own; Peirce's object is not something outside language, in the metaphysical 'substance' that transcends Semiotics, but rather that segment of the content plane which is correlated with a particular expression. Peirce's definition, therefore, does not take us outside the dictionary, which lists the correlations of expression and content available to us as members of a particular language-community or culture. Semiotics is coextensive, it bears repeating, with the field of culture, and in Eco's words, 'an expression does not designate an object but is the bearer of a cultural content'.[14]

In addition to symbols, Peirce recognizes two other

broad classes of signs in which the relation between expression and content is no longer 'unmotivated'. The first of these classes is the *index*: a 'sign which refers to the object that it denotes by virtue of having been really affected by that object'.[15] With an *index* there *is* a natural connection between expression and content. Many indices involve purely natural sequences of cause and effect: as when a 'ring round the sun' is said to be a 'sign' of rain, or smoke to be a sign of fire. Similarly, broken glass on a roadway may be the sign of a recent accident. These three signs are all, in Peircean terms, indexical; expression is linked to content by various physical, i.e. natural laws. But this natural determination does not stop such signs being also cultural and acquiring a different value according to the norms of the culture concerned. A 'ring round the sun' is only one of a number of meteorological signs portending rain, and it may or may not prevail in a given culture. Whether or not it does, whoever uses it in a semic act may so so for practical reasons, if he is a farmer, or for more loosely communicative ones, to display perhaps an acquaintance with weather-lore. An index, for all the natural motivation it incorporates, is open to interpretation like any other sign. It is far from exhausted by serving merely as an index.

The third and last of Peirce's main classes of signs is the *icon*. This is

> a sign which refers to the object that it denotes merely by virtue of characters of its own, and which it possesses just the same, whether any such object exists or not ... Anything whatever, be it quality, existent individual or law, is an icon of anything in so far as it is like that thing and used as a sign of it.[16]

There is thus a picture-element in an *icon*, which is why Peirce chose the term. The relation of expression to content is one of physical similarity. As an iconic sign one might instance the digital V-sign used so successfully by Winston Churchill during World War II.[17] This sign, made by holding the first and second fingers of the hand pointing upwards and away from the body at face height, was iconic of the initial letter of the word Victory. It was a sign of a sign. But for all its iconicity it was highly conventional, the proof of which is that no one could have interpreted it successfully without explanation. It required institutionalization to function as a sign.

Refinements of Peirce's relatively simple tripartite division of signs – and some signs may well be 'mixed' rather than pure examples of one class or another – are possible, but they will be ignored here. The distinction between symbols, indices and icons is all that the amateur semiotician needs to understand the principles and even the practice of Semiotics. There is one more item of terminology which I shall bring in from Peirce, however, because it is useful, and that is the term *interpretant*. This is useful for emphasizing that it is of the essence of any sign, of whatever form, that it be interpretable in accordance with prevailing conventions. The *interpretant* is the name Peirce gives to the response to a particular sign (and not, note, to the interpre*ter* of the sign: the *interpretant* is not a person). The *interpretant* of the Churchillian V-sign is, let us say, an assurance that 'We shall win the war in the end'. Such a string of words may not have been explicitly formulated by those witnessing the V-sign but it is one they might have produced if pressed actually to declare their interpretation of the sign. The semiotician, of course, can deal only in idealizations, and not with the infinitely many unique shades of difference in response to the one sign among individuals.

The important thing is that the *interpretant* of one sign turns out to be more signs. This remains true even if the response to Churchill's V-sign is a smile, bravely worn amidst the wreckage of a bombed street, because this induced smile is a conventional index (or symbol? for do we know for certain that a smile is a *natural* manifestation of the feeling we call 'cheerfulness'?) and will be recognized as such by others. The response of these others to the brave smile then becomes its *interpretant*; and so on *ad infinitum*. The sequence of signs and *interpretants* is unending, involving us in what Eco delightedly calls 'a process of UNLIMITED SEMIOSIS'[18] (his capitals). The process is a little like being trapped inside a dictionary or, as Eco would rather and rightly have it, an encyclopedia, where it is feasible in principle to implicate the whole of human knowledge in the definition of a single sign.

If one blends the sets of terms used by Peirce and by Hjelmslev, one can divide the 'semic act' into its three constituents: expression, content and interpretant. These three constituents are all, very emphatically, in the public domain and not in that of the psychology of the individuals concerned. They are the abstract objects of a *langue* realized in particular acts of *parole*, which is to say, not for the first time in this book, that the means by which we signify are provided for us and not created by us. What we bring to them is the will to employ them in communication. In the words of the phenomenological philosopher Merleau-Ponty: 'Organised signs have their immanent meaning, which depends not on "I think" but on "I can".'[19] This insertion of the individual will into the impersonal system which pre-exists the self, but through which alone human beings can communicate, is the deepest and most vexed problem in Semiotics as in Structuralism, and it is one which will be discussed more directly in the Conclusion to the present study.

Semioticians write frequently of the systems of signs they study as 'codes', even though the term has its ambiguities. What is common to all codes is their artificiality; only those already acquainted with the rules of the code can receive messages in it successfully. Society itself may be presented as a vast and extremely intricate network of codes which enable small or large groups of people within it to communicate their meanings. Even within the largest and most pervasive of all codes, the native language of a population, there are numerous sub-codes, or conventional means of conveying information to some rather than all one's addressees. We should remember that when we speak with each other we employ signs additional to the linguistic signs themselves in order to intensify or expand the meaning of our words: stress, intonation and cadence are all familiar devices in conversation and we can use them successfully only if we observe the rules governing their use. So long as we do that, these devices are conventional and belong to a recognized semiotic system. If we say to someone in English 'You didn't fool *me*', laying stress on the last word of the phrase, we are in no doubt of being understood as we want to be. We are observing a convention which some linguists would allow was a properly linguistic one, fit to be employed even if our addressee is a young child or a foreigner as yet ignorant of it. (In writing English, the same content can be expressed differently, by the use of italic letters, as above; this is a reminder that a language, in Structuralist thought, is an abstract object, not to be confused with the actual physical forms it may take – we none of us think of written and spoken English as two different languages, but as two forms of the one language.) Word stresses we may use which are wholly idiosyncratic, like some – though not all – of the physical gestures people employ in speaking, fall outside any code and are not susceptible of a correct interpretation except fortuitously. All codes are in constant flux, like any other system of signs, and gestures or linguistic usages which begin by being uncoded may eventually be accepted into the code; the systems which semioticians deal with are thus dynamic, being open like all structures to constant elaboration as well as degradation. The considerable extension to our powers of communication which semiotic systems such as those of gesture or intonation represent is one, interestingly, quite absent from our dictionaries. We have no authority to which we can refer to settle questions about which gestures or intonations are conventional and which are not. As users of these linguistic aids we presume that all of them signify, but we should remember that if they are not part of a recognized code their meaning is at best ambiguous.

This dramatic extension of the semiotic field, to include the whole of culture, is looked on by those suspicious of it as a kind of intellectual terrorism, overfilling our lives with meanings. There are more cautious semioticians who take to be signs only those cultural phenomena which declare themselves to be signs: traffic signals, printers' marks, ships' flags, and a vast many other such systems. It is possible and may be profitable to study these systems purely from the syntactical point of view: the systematicity of many such codes could quite certainly be improved by semiotic 'engineering', as one soon realizes when considering road signs from the semiotic point of view – they are a muddle of symbols, indices and icons. (An arduous but revealing test would be to redesign our present system or non-system of road signs so that all of them were iconic and thus potentially universal.)

However, there is no doubt but that it is Semiotics in its wider sense, which takes the whole of culture as its domain, that is the richer, more important study. Like the social anthropology of Lévi-Strauss it observes a sharp dividing-line between the cultural and the natural and believes that everything falling on the cultural side of the divide is open to interpretation, in order to assess its social 'value'. This may be the case even with a phenomenon as 'purely' biological as breathing, an ingenious example picked on by the linguist Sapir.

> Ordinarily the characteristic rhythm of breathing of a given individual is looked upon as a matter for strictly individual definition. But if the emphasis shifts to the consideration of a certain manner of breathing as due to good form or social tradition . . . then the whole subject of breathing at once ceases to be a merely individual concern and takes on the appearance of a social pattern.[20]

The terminology here may not be semiotic, because Sapir would have claimed only to be an anthropologist, but his insight into the unsuspected intrusions of culture on nature is pure Semiotics. As soon as some variation becomes possible in the manner in which we breathe, breathing becomes a more than merely functional process. The semiotics of breathing is never likely to be a very compelling study, even among health faddists, but because of the necessity and universality of the phenomenon it makes an excellent example of the unsuspected intrusiveness of culture in our lives.

Semiotics of this wide-ranging kind has to do with ideologies and how they are transmitted throughout societies. By concentrating as they must on the means and the process of such transmission, semioticians should become unusually alert to the richness of content of often quite familiar and unobtrusive expressions. This was a realization reached in the 1920s in post-Revolutionary Russia by the remarkable linguist and literary 'anthropologist' Mikhail Bakhtin, from whose lead there has descended a whole Russian school of cultural semioticians. Bakhtin, who was primarily but far from exclusively a student of literature, expected to find material evidence of the various ideologies competing in any society in every kind of cultural manifestation. Indeed, this was for him the *only* evidence discoverable for the existence of ideologies, which are not private and immaterial forces in social life but public, concrete ones: 'We are most inclined to imagine ideological creation as some inner process of understanding, comprehension, and perception, and do not notice that it in fact unfolds externally, for the eye, the ear, the hand. It is not within us, but between us.'[21] This is the point of view of a student of society who has truths to tell us about the nature of signification and communication of which we should otherwise be altogether unaware. Bakhtin was not an orthodox Marxist because he revelled in the coexistence, not to say the competition of different ideologies within the same society, but he was Marxist enough to want to 'demystify' society for us and materialist enough to refuse to recognize the existence of ideas except in the form of the signs passing between the members of the society.

Bakhtin thus installs a potent tradition of Semiotics as 'revelation' and of the semiotician as the anthropologically minded observer best capable of 'reading' society on our behalf. It is not essential that a semiotician of this kind should have strong political or social beliefs of his own, though it is likely that he will and that these beliefs will be radical. The danger of Semiotics practised for such 'revelatory' ends is that it will seek to present society as a conspiracy, whereby the hidden meanings found in cultural manifestations by the informed observer are interpreted as the attempts by one class to coerce others or to preserve their hegemony. However, the risk of Semiotics being thus 'loaded' are well worth taking, for it is clear that semioticians may also practise their art in a more or less neutral spirit just like any other social anthropologist.

Unquestionably the most spectacular practitioner of Semiotics as a political 'reading' of society was Roland Barthes, whose training, like Bakhtin's, was mainly in literature. Barthes's book of 1957, *Mythologies*, is a wonderfully acute and sardonic essay in the interpretation of a number of French cultural phenomena from a near-Marxist point of view. At that stage in his life Barthes was inclined to see society in the predatory terms of Marxist analysis, with the bourgeoisie preying malevolently on a repressed proletariat (a view he greatly softened later when he came to appreciate, again like Bakhtin, the virtues of pluralism and of open competition between ideologies). For the Barthes of *Mythologies* semiosis is hygiene, it brings to light the abusive way in which signs can be used by one powerful social group at the expense of others. He uses the term 'myth' in a deliberately tendentious way to refer to such systematic abuse of the process of signification. According to Barthes there are no limits as to which objects may be so abused:

> Anything, therefore, can be a myth? I believe it can, for the universe is infinitely suggestive. Every object in the world may

pass from an enclosed, mute existence to a spoken state, open
to appropriation by society, for no law, natural or not, forbids
us to speak of things. A tree is a tree. But a tree spoken by
Minou Drouet [a celebrated French child poet of the time] is
no longer altogether a tree, but a decorated tree, adapted for a
certain consumption, invested with literary frills, images,
revolts, in short with a social *usage* which is added to the pure
substance.[22]

When he came to propound the theory of his Semiotics,
in order to justify his brilliant practice of it, Barthes relied
heavily on Hjelmslev, and in particular on Hjelmslev's
brief remarks distinguishing semiotic systems which denote
from those which also connote. Barthes himself was a
student of connotations, not of denotations. The difference,
as Hjelmslev puts it, is that a connotative sign-system is
one in which the expression plane is already a sign-system.
This is most easily understood by taking language as the
example: as a sign-system studied by a linguist, language
denotes, it correlates expressions and contents; but once
this basic denotative function is supplanted, as it is in the
case of a literary use of language, the denotative system
becomes the expression of a content to be determined by
the reader. Minou Drouet, or any other literary user of
language, does not 'speak' trees for the denotative purpose
of telling us that such is the sign for that particular object,
but for some literary, i.e., cultural purpose. The poet's tree
is turned, willy-nilly, into what Barthes declares to be a
'fragment of ideology'[23] because it represents a certain
evaluation of trees common to a particular grouping in
society. Trees, since Romanticism at least, are 'poetic';
they are 'natural' – hence the irony of their choice by
Barthes as instances of the cultural. 'Naturalness', as
opposed to artificiality, or 'rurality' as opposed to urbanity,
these are valid *connotations* of the sign 'tree' in the context of
a child's poem, along with the connotation of 'poeticalness',
since it is the characteristic of children's poetry to reflect
very faithfully the commonly accepted view of what objects
or themes are and are not 'poetic'. It is usually possible to

reach a consensus on some at least of the ideological connotations of such signs, though different students of language or semiotics may give different readings of them. Connotations must always be open to argument. In practice Semiotics should encourage freedom in the interpretation of culture, while recognizing that interpretations with which no one else concurs must be deemed to have failed.

Barthes was one of those who believe that Semiotics has to take its lead from linguistics, a view unpopular among those semioticians who, for example, have specialized in the study of animal communication, since it is clear that for all the startling elaborateness of the means some animal species have for passing messages – bees, for example, whose 'dance' movements communicate the distance and direction of pollen sources – they fall very far short of having a true language. But Barthes went further in prophesying that:

> the future no doubt lies in a linguistics of connotation, because, starting with the primary system provided for it by natural language, society is constantly developing systems of second meanings, and this elaboration, which is sometimes openly avowed and at others masked or rationalised, comes close to being a true historical anthropology.[24]

The effect of Barthesian Semiotics is to invest every moment and event in a culture with a significance beyond the simply functional. If we have but the time and the will to seek, the evidence of ideology is pervasive, even if the vast majority of those who are members of the culture live their lives unaware of how their behaviour may be 'read'. Barthes insists that the functional itself inescapably signifies because it is also social: 'as soon as there is society, every usage is converted into a sign of that usage'.[25] Thus the food we eat or the clothes we wear are functional inasmuch as they nourish us or protect us from the elements, but it would be naïve to think that their function exhausts their social 'value'. Both food and clothing are richly invested with connotations; indeed, they might be thought of as being of central interest to the kind of anthropology on which Barthes was engaged, given the variety they display. If there is variation in the way that we breathe, there is a very much greater variation in the way that we eat or dress.

When it comes to evaluating the role of Semiotics itself within society there is a telling convergence between the expansive tradition represented by Barthes and the more cautious, methodical tradition stemming from Peirce. Barthes presents himself as the lucid observer able to instruct citizens less aware than himself in the ways of reading the signs around them and coming to see how a society's meanings may be manipulated by 'decision groups'. Thus a proper understanding of Semiotics will make for a healthier because better educated and 'demystified' society. In the American tradition, Peirce's most influential follower, Charles Morris, looks on Semiotics similarly as a crucial part of the education of the young:

> ... a truly democratic society would aim, as a matter of principle, to enlarge and diversify the sign capacities and resources of its members ... Only in such a society would semiotic(s) be given a basic place in the educational process, so that the individual would be prepared to resist the exploitation of himself by other users of signs, to avoid pathic signs in his behavior, and to make his contribution to the constant correction and creation of signs upon which a healthy society depends.[26]

Morris's remarkable suggestion that the semiotically educated person might avoid 'pathic signs' in his behaviour brings me to the final consideration of this chapter: which is the place of semiotics and hence of Structuralism within psychoanalysis. If semiosis may be said to have begun, practically speaking, in the ancient Greek study of medical symptoms, then it is fitting to end this brief survey with another, contemporary medical application of the discipline. The claim has been made that all mental illnesses or disturbances can be described as defects of the sufferer's semic or signifying powers. This claim is surely too sweeping. But a number of familiar mental conditions can be described in semiotic terms because they affect the linguistic performance of the victim and may end in the collapse of his or her communicative capacity. If a 'semic act' is essentially shared between the two parties to it, then its integrity is threatened if one of those parties is semically incompetent and fails to use the common signs – of the language, let us suppose – in an approved way. The loss is one of sociability.

The psychotherapist's role is to restore sociability and restore semically incapacitated patients to a full or sufficient communicability with others. The therapist is faced, in performing this role, with signs which he has been trained to identify as symptoms, in the form of bodily malfunctions without apparent organic cause or behavioural malfunctions such as compulsions, disturbing dreams, severe inhibitions, irrational phobias and so on. These are the expressions for which the analyst is expected to locate the content. As presented by the patient, the symptoms are either without content or have been given a content with which the psychoanalyst will be dissatisfied, believing that their 'real' content is other than what it appears to be. This, anyway, is the Freudian model, which is of the greatest moment from any semiotic viewpoint. The task of the Freudian analyst is to recover contents that have been successfully 'repressed' by the patient, in a pattern strongly reminiscent of that to be found in the work of Barthes, who in *Mythologies* is dealing very much with ideological symptoms which remain latent until the trained interpreter of them appears.

The Freudian psychoanalyst is thus the very model of a semiotician. Freud's own description of the method which he evolved was that, in its early days, 'Psychoanalysis was above all an art of interpretation'.[27] It has remained so, despite the shift which Freud introduced whereby the responsibility for the interpretation of symptoms passed from doctor to patient; by thus inviting the patient to 'experience' the 'true' meaning of his symptoms the analyst hopes to achieve a cure. This notion, again, is very close to that held by buoyant semioticians such as Morris, that in accurate semiosis there is health, for individuals in the first instance and hence for society as a whole.

In semiotic terms Freud extended the area of recognized significance in human life quite dramatically, by bringing people to admit as signs phenomena which would previously have been thought trivial or even meaningless. The jokes, slips of the tongue or pen, and dreams which are the staple of a well-known kind of Freudian analysis or 're-reading' have all been charged with a new, if often debatable significance. What is of concern to Semiotics, or to Structuralism, is not the nature of the interpretations which Freudianism specializes in but the methods it employs to produce them. A premise of these methods is that such 'symptoms' as a dream, or an act of forgetfulness, are not interpretable as isolated entities but as events within a certain psychic system, the relations between whose parts are of the essence to Freudian thought. Freud's model of the human psyche cannot be accused of being atomistic, when he stressed so often that it was 'topographical', dynamic or even 'economic', metaphors all of them bringing out his underlying premise of a psychic *structure* existing in each one of us. The old idea of the Self as a unitary principle or force that is absolute master in its own bodily house has found it hard to recover from Freud's tripartite division of the psyche into Ego, Id and Superego; these three elements would certainly seem to form a structure since they are unthinkable in independence one of the others and are constituted by the relations which join them. Their respective 'values' within any individual shift constantly, and psychic 'health' is taken to depend on their preserving a certain equilibrium. On the other hand, the three elements or 'terms' of this particular structure are normally seen hierarchically, not as equals: it is our inclination to look on the Ego as a term superior to the other two, and our psychic structure, therefore, as having a 'centre'. We are not prepared for a truly Structuralist access of egalitarianism, which would 'de-centre' our Selves altogether.

If Freudianism, both professional and popular, has flourished, this is because of the shock effects it is well capable of producing in associating unexpected contents with seemingly innocent expressions. A dramatic and also dynamic element is brought into semiosis by the notion of repression. Repression it is which distorts the healthy semic function and which converts banal signs into puzzles. The psychoanalyst, who knows or claims to know how correctly to solve these puzzles for us, brings both understanding and sanity in one. In *The Interpretation of Dreams*, which is one of this century's masterworks in the methods of semiosis, Freud describes the analyst's role in quasi-linguistic terms:

> We are thus presented with a new task which had no previous existence: the task, that is, of investigating the relations between the manifest content of dreams and the latent dream-thoughts, and of tracing out the process by which the latter have been changed into the former.
>
> The dream-thoughts and the dream-content are presented to us like two versions of the same subject-matter in two different languages. Or, more properly, the dream-content seems like a transcript of the dream-thoughts into another mode of expression, whose characters and syntactic laws it is our business to discover by comparing the original and the translation.[28]

Freudianism is semiosis at its most seductive, inasmuch as it offers us therapeutic solutions to what might otherwise remain distressing psychic mysteries, but also at its most coercive, since the latent contents elucidated by Freudian interpretation seldom seem open to argument. But from any Structuralist point of view, Freudianism, be it successful in therapeutic terms or not, and plausible in its specific interpretations or not, is of importance because of the essential reliance which it places on the function of language in our lives, and more especially on the restrictions on complete self-expression which any such sign-system necessarily imposes. It is linguistic through and through because it is founded on the exchange of words between patient and doctor, or what in their more optimistic moments psychoanalysts may refer to as 'the talking cure'.

The psychoanalyst who has done most to bring out the dependence of Freud's thought and method on language, and the convergence between Freudianism and Structuralism, is the Frenchman Jacques Lacan, a Surrealist poet turned analyst. Lacan saw himself as the man who would purge Freudianism of false accretions and misreadings and return to the pure doctrine, but unfortunately he carried out this programme in a prose of such flamboyance and syntactic oddity that few can follow it with ease and many cannot follow it at all. The consequence has been that the figure of Lacan himself interposes over-strongly between Freud and those looking to Lacan for a faithful account of Freud's writings. However, it is through Lacan that the Freudian current has flowed once and for all into Structuralism or, if one prefers, that the Structuralist current has flowed into Freudianism.

The overall effect of Lacan's writings and teachings has been to assert more strongly than ever before the linguistic basis of psychoanalysis. There are many who doubt that 'the talking cure' is really curative, but there can be none, especially since Lacan, who doubt that it can be talkative. As a student of Saussure as well as of Freud, Lacan is committed to seeing the manifest and latent planes of verbal or other sign-behaviour as continuous with each other, and both as being structured like a language. We may be tempted to think of Freud's 'dream-thoughts', for instance, as lying outside or beyond language, even though that would be to deem them incommunicable. But *whatever* enters into the exchange between patient and analyst participates for Lacan in what he calls the 'symbolic order', for the good semiotic reason that without symbols (signs) there can be no communication. Patient and analyst meet, like any two other individuals who share a sign-system, within the symbolic order, even though the symbols they exchange do not exhaust the contents of their psyche: the uncommunicated or ineffable remains as what cannot find admission to the 'symbolic order' but is the unique psychic possession of the individual. This inexpressible realm is not to be identified with the unconscious, because the Lacanian unconscious *can* be brought to expression; it is that which is either missing from the exchange between patient and analyst or that which enters the exchange in a perverted form: 'The unconscious is that chapter of my story which is marked by a blank or occupied by a falsehood: it is the censored chapter. But the truth can be rediscovered; most often it is already written elsewhere.'[29]

This 'elsewhere' will be some other part of the patient's behaviour and by 'written' Lacan means open to successful interpretation by the vigilant analyst. It is as if a person's acts constituted a 'text' and the analyst's job was to render that 'text' coherent, despite its various gaps, illogicalities and so on.

Lacan makes explicit use of Saussure's model of linguistic sign and its division into a signifier and a signified. In the *Course in General Linguistics* the relation of signifier to signified is given in the form of a diagram:[30]

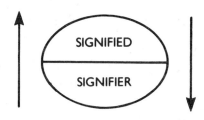

This simple but crucial representation of what in this chapter I have called the 'semiotic function' is described by Lacan as the Saussurean 'algorithm'. But Lacan deliberately misrepresents Saussure's diagram. Where Saussure has placed the signified above the signifier, or the content above the expression, Lacan does the opposite. He redesigns the 'algorithm' thus: $\frac{S}{s}$. Here the upper and larger of the two Ss stands for the signifier and the lower and smaller for the signified. Lacan's version of the diagram, therefore, sets a higher store by the signifier than by the signified, and in so doing reproaches Saussure and his followers for their presumed idealism; if we accept, that is, that by drawing his diagram as he did Saussure intended us to think that the content somehow preceded its expression. (This interpretation depends on our assuming that the symbol which appears above the dividing-line is 'superior' to the lower one in more than merely topological terms). Lacan, on the contrary, is set on removing 'the illusion that the signifier answers to the function of representing the signified'.[31] The Freudian doctrine, as he repeats and elaborates it, is that there is above all 'slippage' between signifiers and signifieds, and that the 'bar' which separates them in Saussure's diagram is itself functional, since whenever there is some 'pathic' disturbance of the semiotic function the bar can be taken as representing the censorship exercised by the unconscious. The censorship divorces signifiers from their 'true' signifieds and frees them to function as it were privately rather than in their usual public function. It is as if the planes of expression and content were separated by a clutch mechanism which grants the first a limited but highly significant independence from the second. Lacan's authority for this view he gets from Freud and from Freud's discoveries concerning the 'transcription' of 'dream-thoughts' into 'dream-content'. Freud's explanation of how one is turned into the other depends greatly on the 'syntactical' operations that he calls 'condensation' and 'displacement'. 'Condensation' occurs whenever a single signifier or expression in the manifest 'dream-content' is shown by analysis to have multiple signifieds or contents in the latent 'dream-thoughts' (this disproportion is often known as 'over-determination'); and 'displacement' occurs whenever what the analyst believes to be the 'true' content of a manifest expression is found in other than its rightful place in the sequence of such expressions, lurking, that is, behind a false signifier. It is Lacan's belief that discoveries of this sort, which involve the dream analyst in a redistribution of expressions and contents, justify him in his 'literalism' and in his elevating the signifier to a precedence over the signified. For the signifier is all that the analyst has to go on, it is what is actually *there*, either in the form of the patient's words or of some other item of behaviour. The content of that expression is not pre-determined, in these 'pathic' instances, by the code common to patient and analyst and to all other members of the sign-community; though it may, of course, be pre-determined by the sub-code adopted by Freudians to deal with such semiotic malfunctions.

The important lesson for Semiotics to come from the practice of psychoanalysis is of the ease with which we can all, 'pathic' cases or not, deviate from the codes we inherit and use as members of our society. Psychoanalysis attempts to repair extreme cases of such deviance, where it has caused unhappiness; semiotics can limit itself to showing how deviance works and how it depends ultimately on the 'encyclopedic' nature of the content plane of language. Far from being coercive, Semiotics should be libertarian, in pointing to the infinite richness of interpretation which linguistic signs at least are open to; and pointing also to Lacan's typically paradoxical truth of: 'the possibility I have, precisely to the extent that my language is common to me and to other subjects ... to use it to signify something quite other from what it says.'[32] That is, we can lie, romance and deceive (ourselves as well as others) because the expression plane of our language is so very economical and hence ambiguous. Which dark thought is entirely suited to stand here, as the transition to a chapter on the applications of Structuralism and Semiotics to the study of Literature.

NOTES

1. See the brief comments on this by Dan Sperber in *Structuralism and Since*, ed. J. Sturrock, pp. 23–4.
2. Some symptoms may also *be* the illness; the marks on the skin which turn out to be the condition known as eczema themselves constitute the condition. Are we wrong in such instances to take the signs to be 'symptoms'?

3. U. Eco, *Trattato di semiotica generale*, p. 30.

4. T. Hobbes, *Leviathan*, p. 16.

5. J. Locke, *An Essay Concerning Human Understanding*, p. 354.

6. Saussure, *Course in General Linguistics*, pp. 15–16.

7. C. S. Peirce, *Collected Writings*, Vol. 5, p. 448n.

8. L. Hjelmslev, *Prolégomènes à une théorie du langage*, p. 98.

9. L. Wittgenstein, *Philosophical Investigations*, p. 269.

10. Eric Buyssens, *La Communication et l'articulation linguistique*, p. 11.

11. G. Mounin, *Introduction à la sémiologie*, p. 12.

12. Confusion may occur because of the different usages of the term 'symbol' by Saussure and by Peirce. Peirce's definition is precise and is the one generally adopted; Saussure's usage is loose because he did not have any typology of signs. He uses the term 'symbol' as it is still widely used in English today, to refer to those signs which we recognize to be 'symbolic': the cross as the symbol of Christianity, the Union Jack as the symbol of Britain, and so on.

13. Peirce, op. cit., Vol. 2, p. 143.

14. Eco, op. cit., p. 91.

15. Peirce, op. cit., Vol. 2, p. 143.

16. *Ibid.*, p. 143.

17. The Churchillian V-sign is also a parody, to complicate matters further, being a polite adaptation of the ruder kind of V-sign still widely used in Britain. The Churchillian adaptation, effected by reversing the position of the fingers so that the knuckles face inwards instead of outwards, will have been 'read' additionally as being a V-sign of the older kind directed against Hitler and against Nazi Germany.

18. Eco, op. cit., p. 101.

19. M. Merleau-Ponty, *Eloge de la philosophie*, p. 93.

20. Quoted in *Edward Sapir: Appraisals of his Life and Work*, p. 90.

21. M. Bakhtin and P. Medvedev, *The Formal Method in Literary Scholarship*, p. 8.

22. R. Barthes, *Mythologies*, p. 216.

23. Barthes, *Eléments de sémiologie*, p. 165.

24. *Ibid.*, p. 164.

25. *Ibid.*, p. 113.

26. C. Morris, *Writings on the General Theory of Signs*, p. 289.

27. S. Freud, *Beyond the Pleasure Principle*, p. 17.

28. Freud, *The Interpretation of Dreams*, p. 277.

29. J. Lacan, *Ecrits, Tome 1*, p. 136.

30. Saussure, op. cit., p. 113.

31. Lacan, op. cit., p. 255.

32. *Ibid.*, p. 262.

4
LITERATURE

Literary Structuralism is Structuralism in its most provocative and unpopular form. Structural linguists and anthropologists, and semioticians, may not carry all their colleagues with them but the disagreements they meet with are seldom bitter; but those specialists in literature who have adopted Structuralist ways of analysis have often had a hard time of it. This is because there are many concerned with the making and teaching of literature who believe that Structuralism is a damagingly narrow and mechanistic way of understanding literary texts, that it reduces literature to a largely impersonal technique instead of the superior form of self-expression we ordinarily hold it to be. Certainly Structuralism undermines the naïve but endemic view that literature, like other art-forms, is essentially self-expression, because of its insistence that one 'self' may be mediated to another only by means of a common, objective system of signs. In the case of literature, the objective system which authors necessarily have recourse to is two-fold: there is the system of their native language itself and the system, overlaid on that, of characteristically 'literary' conventions to which they must also accede if they are to achieve recognizably literary works. By giving its attention to these objective aspects of literature, situated between author and reader, Structuralism corrects what it sees as an old, deep-rooted imbalance in literary-critical thought which emphasizes the uniqueness of both texts and authors. Each text and author *is* unique, but in order to decide what this uniqueness is one needs to understand the literary 'system' within which they exist. Different texts and authors have much more in common than may be supposed, and Structuralism tries to bring this out. It is in search of the *langue* of which each individual literary work is the *parole*.

This would seem a modest programme, not calculated to give offence to anybody. Structuralism above all should be able to live in peace with its neighbours because to a true Structuralist all the alternative modes of conducting literary criticism form a single system and the 'value' of any one of them is determined by its relations with the others. That there has been antagonism towards Structuralism in the literary field has been due partly to the aggressive and obscurantist way in which some Structuralists have tried to make their case, and partly to the fear felt by many who are not Structuralists that the triumph of Structuralism would be the death of 'humanism' in literature. This fear is unfounded. All that Structuralism proposes to do is to establish the limits within which subjectivity must work.

Literary Structuralism is not the novelty which its opponents claim it to be. It is, rather, the latest, unusually sophisticated stage reached by a form of literary criticism that has existed since Aristotle. Just as Aristotle, in his *Poetics*, set out to codify the literary genre of tragedy as it was practised in Ancient Greece, so any literary Structuralist today wants to identify the very many rules and conventions informing the practice of literature in general. He seeks the system of which individual texts are the 'events'. The process is one of abstraction and of comparison between texts, since it is only by comparing texts perceived as belonging to the one system that their invariant elements can be determined. Structuralism might well call itself Poetics, indeed, if it were not for the implication that that term applies only to poetry. Contemporary Structuralism goes beyond the sort of Poetics one finds in Aristotle, but it starts from the desire to know how literature is made. We are all better off, as readers, for knowing something of the rules which literature follows (or breaks) and for recognizing to what extent those who write must yield to the literary system if they are to do so meaningfully. A certain amount of Structuralism is, or should be, a part of any literary education.

Even if Poetics has a long history, it is in the present century that it has come to the fore as a literary study, and a proper account of literary Structuralism needs to begin with the first concerted effort at redirecting attention to the structural aspects of literature. This was made between about 1915 and 1930 by the Russian Formalists. The Formalists had begun to elaborate their ideas before the Russian Revolution broke out in 1917, but they flourished especially in the revolutionary atmosphere of the 1920s, when it was thought right and exciting to overturn all the old orthodoxies, in literary as in other thought. Later, Formalism went dangerously out of favour with the hard-line Marxists who dominated intellectual life in Russia and it more or less disappeared from public view. Its followers, however, survived Stalin's purges, and Russian Formalism reappeared, in a more explicitly semiotic form, in the 1960s and after; its links with Western Structuralism have not been close but there is a strong convergence of ideas between the two.

Formalism, like the Structuralism that descends from it, represents not an occasional but a permanent option for the student of literature: it is the theoretical pole of the literary consciousness, one might say. The Formalists in Russia were preoccupied with the techniques and conventions of literature because their critical predecessors in that country had ignored them. The 'Symbolists' and 'Aesthetes' from whom the Formalists took over had worried about literature's 'message' or about its 'beauty'. To Formalism these were dead terms, against which it reacted with great vigour. The Formalists were young and iconoclastic, as many Structuralists have been, and what they proposed was to break away from the genteel, over-personal styles of criticism prevalent among their elders and to replace these with something much tougher and more objective. This, they believed, would put them in tune with the times. Taken to extremes, Formalism can come to look like a 'science' of literature, propounding axioms that are beyond argument. But such scientism is never welcome in literary circles which prize – and rightly – freedom of interpretation. Formalism often went too far, because it was polemical; if it hadn't gone too far, it might not have gone far enough. And the same can be said of Structuralism.

The starting-point for Formalism is the insistence that literature be studied as literature and not as a branch of some other discipline – of psychology, say, or sociology. Authors may and do psychologize and sociologize, but that is a side-issue: it is not of the essence of literature. Formalism lays immense store by the 'specificity' of literature, or those peculiar features of literary texts which it was the critic's job to discover and to classify. In the words of a leading Formalist, B. M. Eichenbaum: 'What does characterise us is the endeavour to create an autonomous discipline of literary studies based on the specific properties of literary material.'[1] This notion, of literature forming an autonomous field, with its own laws, echoes closely the Saussurean view of language (though Saussure's work was quite unknown to the Formalists, at least in the early days).

From its beginnings Russian Formalism brought the study of literature close together with the study of language. Some Formalists, Roman Jakobson notably, were students of philology and already extremely erudite in linguistic terms. They saw literature as a particular use of language and condemned earlier critics who had written of literary matters as if the language itself were transparent and negligible, because only the transcendent 'message' counted. Some of the Formalists were friendly with the most technically progressive writers of the day in Russia, with the Futurists and the so-called 'trans-sense' or 'trans-rational' poets. 'Trans-sense' poetry was poetry in which the poet attended solely to the sounds and the other formal features of his verses, with the result that their meanings were either obscure or, at worst (or best?) non-existent. Khlebnikov, the 'trans-sense' poet whom Jakobson esteemed above all other Russian poets of this century, saw his role as being to worry himself about the signifiers and let the signifieds take care of themselves. Euphonious non-sense is the ideal product of such a technique, or 'verbal music' as it can more flatteringly be called. The poet becomes very conspicuously the servant of the medium in which he is working rather than appearing to make it do his bidding. Taken a step further, the technique turns into the 'automatic writing' of the Surrealists, who abandon all creative prerogatives, as normally understood, and allow their writing to be 'dictated' by their subconscious.

Poetry such as Khlebnikov's was a major contribution to what another prominent Formalist, Viktor Shklovsky, referred to excitedly as the 'resurrection of the word'. Previously, readers had been expected to see 'through' the word, now they would have to pause and look *at* it. If you invent words, as Khlebnikov did, by extrapolation from the existing stock, you attract a reader's attention to the individual term and pose the problem of its meaning. As much as a 'resurrection' of the word, such a technique reveals a 'materialism' of the word, which strikes us first of all by its opacity.

The procedure does more than just recognize the autonomy of literature in respect of reality: it *flaunts* it, as it is flaunted in English literature's most extraordinary 'trans-sense' achievement, James Joyce's *Finnegans Wake*. But the shift from the signified to the signifier as the apparent focus of the author's attention may lead to anxiety and suspicion on the part of the reader. Authors like Joyce and Khlebnikov are deplored for playing 'games' with us; the texts which they leave to us contain all too many puzzles, stemming from a culpable authorial abdication before the forces of language itself. What is 'trans-sense' is never without sense; like *Finnegans Wake* it may be full to overflowing with sense, to the point where critics can spend a lifetime extracting more and more meanings from it. Meaning thus becomes a problem: for Structuralism *the* problem of literature. It has somehow to be contained.

Both Formalism and Structuralism start from an 'immanent' view of the meaning of literary works. That is, they attempt to exclude from consideration whatever is external to the text or texts they are studying. No two students of literature, however, will agree on what is or is not 'external' to the text, since a lot of what we like to think is 'in' the text turns out, on close inspection, to have been brought *to* the text by ourselves. There can be no pure 'immanence' in criticism or interpretation; but this does not stop the principle being a valuable one. It is valuable because it warns us against reverting in textual interpretation to the psychological and sociological modes of old; the 'immanent' reading of a work seeks to exclude as far as possible information about the author or about the society and age in which he or she lived and wrote, unless of course it is contained in the text. The meanings of the text are to be determined within the text itself, by the correlation of its parts: this, I stress, are the meanings *of* the text, and are not to be taken as the full sum of meanings I or any reader may derive from it in reading, many of which will be unique to myself. The point of 'immanence' is to show how any text forms a semantic system of its own, a careful reading of which is a reader's first responsibility. The 'immanentist' critic forbears to argue from textual facts to psychological or sociological ones independent of the text, as is so commonly done by those critics who 'explain' an element in a work by some biographical datum of its author. The 'value' of a textual fact has to be determined textually, according to the place it occupies within its particular system. What an 'immanent' criticism asks is not that we should disqualify all external interpretation of a text for ever and ever but that we should see it as secondary; literary facts are literary *before* they are psychological, historical, and so on.

The thrust of Russian Formalism, then, was to discover

what was peculiar to literature: those features which together constitute 'literariness' as Jakobson calls it. If this 'literariness' is, as it has to be, a function of language, it can be found only differentially. If there is a specifically literary use of language, there must be a non-literary use of it also, from which the literary use can be distinguished. Formalism came to be based on a binary scheme whereby language was divided into the 'poetic' or literary and the 'everyday'. This is a distinction we can most of us recognize, in so far as our own language contains words and turns of phrase which we characterize promptly enough as literary or 'bookish' if we meet with them outside a literary context. However, there are a great many more words and turns of phrase which belong equally to the literary and the everyday language, and those which are conspicuously literary are the very ones which a fastidious author is anxious to avoid when writing. The distinction can never be one of vocabulary or grammar.

Rather, it must be stated in wider, functional terms, as it was by Jakobson. He argues that there are six distinct linguistic functions, any one of which may have precedence in a given situation. For my purposes here I shall single out only the function which Jakobson calls the 'poetic'. This is to be distinguished from the other five functions by the fact that it fixes the attention of the two parties to the communicative act – speaker and hearer; writer and reader – on the actual words which are being used. The focus is on the message, for its own sake. Jakobson does not suggest that the poetic function can operate alone, only that in any literary use of language it is 'dominant' (a key term with the Formalists and one which looks forward to Structuralism, since it entails the existence of a system of functions, any one of which may achieve temporary dominance over the rest).

The poetic function of language has as its effect that when we read literature we become more aware of language than we are when we are confronted by language in its other functions. To introduce another term dear to the

Formalists, in literature language is 'foregrounded'. This, as Jakobson stresses, is the *tendency* of literature, much more fully recognized in poetry than it is in prose. In the everyday use of language it will seldom be practical and may even be found impolite to 'foreground' language. Everyday language is usually informative and instrumental; there is no call for either speaker/writer or hearer/reader to dwell on the form of what is said/written since if a piece of information has been successfully passed or some action successfully instigated, the words by which this has been managed can count as 'transparent'. With the poetic function comes a certain opacity, for the writer is no longer passing information nor seeking to instigate action. There may also come an intentional ambiguity, which is something else we customarily avoid if we can in using language for our everyday purposes since it may very well defeat those purposes or cause them to miscarry. (It is quite possible for the poetic function to be dominant in speech also, though it may be adjudged pretentious by listeners.)

It is not only poetry which is 'poetic', then, but any piece of language, long or short, specifiable as literary. Prose too is 'poetic' and open to the same kind of structural analysis that is perfectly familiar in the case of verse: it was one of the strengths of Russian Formalism, indeed, that it was so eager to investigate narrative prose and determine the laws of its construction – to find, in the typically insolent title of a famous Formalist essay, 'How Gogol's "Overcoat" is made', the 'Overcoat' in question being the title of a story by Gogol. In Formalist terms poetry is like prose only more so: both rely on a distinctive use of language which it is the critic's task to describe. It is sometimes overlooked, however, that it is the *use* of the language and not the language itself which is literary, a point decisively made by Bakhtin and P. M. Medvedev in an early (1929) and profound critique of Formalism when they wrote that: 'Language acquires poetic characteristics only in the concrete poetic construction. These characteristics do not belong to language in its linguistic capacity, but to the construction, whatever its form may be. The most elementary everyday utterance or apt expression may be perceived artistically in certain circumstances.'[2]

This is a statement of 'holism'. Structuralists, I hope, are less likely than the Formalists were to fall into the error Bakhtin and Medvedev are here correcting. It is the whole which determines the parts, and not the parts the whole; only in a 'poetic' or literary whole can the parts be grasped as 'poetic'. The Formalists were adept at identifying the 'devices' on which literature depends, the artifices, that is, able to be employed by a writer for his or her aesthetic purposes. The 'devices' are the means by which the literary use of language departs from the everyday, since they are found in the one and not in the other. Plot, characterization, dialogue, rhyme, rhythm, metaphor: all are examples of 'devices' in either prose or verse, differently used in different periods of literary history or by different authors within the same period. In its early days Formalism was generally content to isolate 'devices', rather than to consider the uses they were put to in particular texts. The ever-polemical Shklovsky declared, notoriously, that: 'A work of literature is the sum-total of all stylistic devices employed in it.'[3] What was missing from this exuberant formulation was any sense that the work of literature had a certain unity, and that it was more than a mere accumulation of specific 'devices' taken by the author from stock.

It is understandable that for a number of years Formalism was content to collect literary 'facts' in this way, because it had not been systematically done before, and such a collection was needed if the 'specificity' of literature was to be characterized. This was sound spadework. But it was not enough because it fails to account for our intuition as readers that a given work, be it narrative or poetic, has unity, that, to go for a second time to the arguments of Bakhtin and Medvedev, it is not only 'made' but also 'created'.[4] To grasp the work as a *structure* restores to it the oneness it might otherwise lose. As a whole, it becomes readily comparable with other wholes, which may be different works by the same author, works by different authors within the same genre, and so on. A structural view of a single text opens the way for wider applications of Structuralism, extensible if need be to whole cultures. The comparisons made possible are between structure and structure, not between one element from one structure and one element from another. The Structuralist position is that it is no good relating this element or that of a fiction, say, to life, but only the whole to which the element belongs, a position that may be generalized in the words of F. W. Galan (writing about Prague Structuralism) that 'In every work of art, in sum, composition holds sway over representation . . .'[5]

Literary Structuralism could not exist in its present form without the preliminary endeavours of the Formalists to bring out the full artificiality of literary art. Formalism, as its name indicates, played down the importance of content in literature, because it thought that earlier critics had accorded it too great a place. Much Formalist criticism is excessive in arguing that the content of literature is only there for the sake of the form, and not the other way about; that a writer's object is to renovate literature formally, by some unprecedented use of 'devices', rather than to 'say' something that has not been said before. It is doubtful whether the Formalists advanced such views quite seriously, but for as long as they continued to hold them it was possible to ignore any question of the unity of works of literary art or of the relation between literature and other contemporary cultural practices.

These were questions which came back into fashion as Formalism evolved into Structuralism, a development which may be said to have happened gradually during the late 1920s and 1930s, very much under the influence of Jakobson and the new group of like-minded linguists, critics and others which had formed around him in Prague. They it was who propounded and to some extent popularized the notion of *system*, which was easily extended from the linguistic sphere to the aesthetic: 'With the further development of Formalism, there arose the accurate conception of a poetic work as a structured system, a regularly ordered hierarchical set of artistic devices.'[6] The two crucial new ideas included here and which were largely missing in the earlier Formalism are those of integration and dynamism, both of which are fundamental to Structuralism. If the poetic work – and 'poetic', remember, is being used in its wider sense to mean any literary text – is now seen as a system, then the parts of the system have to be understood as acting one upon the other, according to rules to be determined; and an alteration in one part of the system will have repercussions throughout it. Moreover, this new definition of the poetic work can be extended way beyond a single text, to include an *oeuvre*, a genre, a whole literature, all of which are quite able to be studied as similarly dynamic wholes. The passage from Formalism to Structuralism enables literature to be reinserted into the societies in which it is produced and read, and to re-enter history. Given the widespread belief that Structuralism is furiously opposed to history, this may seem strange; but it was very much a mark of Prague Structuralism that it set out to integrate literature with other arts and with cultural practices generally. Jakobson contested the extreme synchronism (as he saw it) of Saussure, on the grounds that a purely synchronic system lacked dynamism. He pointed to the dynamics of linguistic change, with rival forms competing for semantic territory until such time as one gives way or is transformed. And Prague Structuralism came to see the synchronic system of a culture as dynamic in the same way, its energy being provided first and foremost by a dialectical contest between the acknowledged norms prevailing in the system and the wish of those using the system to break with them.

With a linguist like Jakobson it was perhaps inevitable that the integration of the literary work should remain a formal one, and to hark back to the 'devices' of the Formalists. In his own essays on literary as opposed to linguistic subjects, Jakobson has specialized in the most dauntingly thorough grammatical analyses of poetry, as if it were possible and fruitful to characterize the work of particular poets according to the use they have made of the grammatical choices open to them: 'The essential literary-critical question of the individuality and comparative characteristics of poems, poets and poetic schools can and should be posed in the realm of grammar.'[7] This was written not in 1921, as one might think, but in 1961. Jakobson continued all his long life to look on the semantic aspects of verse – he had little if anything to say about prose – as coming second to the formal; indeed, as derivative from the formal. In the most resonant public statement he ever made of his views, at an American university conference in 1958, he endorsed with great enthusiasm remarks made by Gerard Manley Hopkins a century earlier to the effect that 'parallelism' was the fundamental problem of poetry, parallelism being that structural principle whereby one element in a piece of verse is perceived as related to another, as with rhyme, alliteration, simile, and so on. Of these formal recurrences Hopkins asserts that their force is 'to beget a recurrence or parallelism answering to it in the words or thought and, speaking roughly and rather for the tendency than the invariable result, the more marked parallelism in structure whether of elaboration or of emphasis begets more marked parallelism in the words and sense.'[8]

This precedence of the 'device' over the sense is one never abandoned by Jakobson in his analyses of particular poems. These, one concludes, are exhaustive, as he counts, classifies and contrasts 'figures of grammar' (also Hopkins's phrase). But the conclusions to be drawn from the grammatical analysis are thin and open to question, if one's concern is to grasp the semantic structure of the poem. Jakobson's method is to establish, like the structural linguist he is, opposed pairings within his grammatical classes, but even where the opposition is semantic rather than purely formal – as when he enumerates and contrasts 'animate' and 'inanimate' nouns in a poem – the results are not especially telling. Their most appealing feature for many Structuralists is that much of the patterning in which Jakobson deals belongs to language, or the system, rather than to the author whose work he is analysing. That is to say, they are patternings of which the author may well have been unconscious. Certainly, he or she is unlikely to have been conscious of the oppositional nature of the structure so created. Jakobson's demonstrations of the unsuspected rigour and regularity of verse structures are impressive and serve to reinforce powerfully the Structuralist view that when we submit, as individuals, to sign-systems we necessarily abdicate something of our individuality. The paradox of poetry has always been that it is at once the most personal and the most constraining of literary forms, and Structuralism such as Jakobson's centres on that paradox.

The paradox is less obvious with literary prose, though it is present just the same. No one questions that prose is less constraining than verse, that the author's freedom of choice is correspondingly greater and that prose structures are thus looser than verse ones. To a Structuralist, prose offers a fresher and harder challenge than poetry, and any successful demonstration of just how highly structured it is will be all the more dramatic. What Structuralists have examined is mainly narrative prose, for the good reason that the structure of a narrative is apparent, whereas that, say, of a literary essay is not. A structural study of the stories of Conan Doyle, which are nearly all narrative, is an altogether more encouraging prospect than one of the essays of Charles Lamb, from which narrative is largely absent. Structuralist study of the other major component of Western fiction (apart from narrative), which is character, has to date been skimpy. Literary Structuralism is open to the charge that it has tackled only what is easiest, and engaged with those structures that stand out from the rest. It must be the case, however, that the grammar and semantics of fictional 'characters' will one day be effectively codified, to the improvement of our understanding of how 'characters' are made, as those of plots have already begun to be.

The pattern for the contemporary study of narrative prose was also set in Russia, in the 1920s, by Vladimir Propp. In 1928 he published a short study called *The Morphology of the Russian Folk-tale*. His aims were both scientific and structural: 'The word morphology signifies the study of forms. In botany, morphology comprises the study of the component parts of plants, and of their relations one to another and to the whole; in other words, the study of the structure of a plant.'[9]

The material with which Propp chose to work was 100 Russian folktales all of which contained some element of the 'marvellous'. The classification of the tales was not his own but one established by folklorists, so he cannot be faulted for choosing his stories to suit himself. Folktales, on the other hand, do have advantages of simplicity for the kind of analysis on which Propp was engaged: the narrative element is all-important, they are patently stereotyped in terms of events and characters, they are clumsily articulated, having been 'made' rather than 'created', and they are anonymous. They are in every respect comparable to the myths analysed by Lévi-Strauss.

To delimit the field of study is the first requirement of Structuralism; Propp's 100 comparable tales form a whole. The second requirement is to define the constituent units of the whole. It might be thought that in this case each folktale represents one unit, and so, at a peculiarly uninteresting level of analysis, it does. To remain at this level is to leave out of account the very strikingly composite nature of each tale. It would be possible to relate the tales one to another as wholes, in structural terms, but more instructive at the outset to define the elements of which each tale is constructed.

Propp's method is to divide the tales up into what he terms 'functions'. These are what an ordinary reader of them would most likely refer to as 'actions', but by redesignating actions as 'functions' Propp has already begun on the necessary Structuralist task of abstraction and generalization. A 'function' is an action seen as lending itself to assimilation to other, comparable actions elsewhere in the corpus of tales. The spotting of such similarities is a sometimes difficult but essential part of any Structuralist approach to literature. Structuralism thrives on the repetitions in which any text abounds, and to this extent Jakobson's principle of 'parallelism' in poetry may be taken as central to prose also. To make clear what form Propp's assimilations take, I will cite four of his own descriptions of actions in different tales, each of which contains two distinct 'functions':

1 The king gives an eagle to a brave man. The eagle carries the brave man off into another kingdom.
2 The grandfather gives a horse to Soutchenko. The horse carries Soutchenko off into another kingdom.
3 A magician gives a boat to Ivan. The boat carries Ivan off into another kingdom.
4 The queen gives a ring to Ivan. Strong men come out of the ring and carry Ivan off into another kingdom.[10]

The assimilations here are made simple by the repetition of the verb-forms 'gives' and 'carries off'. In each of the numbered cases two of Propp's 'functions' are to be identified, one in each sentence of the pair. The function common to the four first sentences is described by Propp as 'Receipt of the magic object', and the function common to the four second sentences as 'Displacement in space between two kingdoms, journey with a guide'. These descriptions pick out the invariant element in each set of four variations. The two functions themselves are in fact the fourteenth and fifteenth in a complete list of thirty-one. From these it is possible to construct all of the tales of the chosen corpus. This is a further instance of the Structuralist principle of economy, so prominent in its philosophy of language; from a limited number of 'functions' an enormous variety of tales can be generated, just as in language a great many words can be made from relatively few phonemes, and an infinite number of sentences from a limited vocabulary.

In the case of the folktales, however, the powers of combination of the 'functions' are limited by other kinds of constraint. There is their syntax to be considered. In a given language some sequences of phonemes do not occur, and would be held by speakers of the language to be impossible or unpronounceable, even if there is no innate physiological reason why that should be so. Similarly, in the case of Propp's narrative 'functions' many combinations will be disallowed on logical grounds. In the instance I have cited, of the fourteenth and fifteenth 'functions', there is an obvious logical constraint inasmuch as no 'displacement in space' can be effected before the magic means of it has been provided. The hero cannot be carried off if his eagle never arrives. Logically, 'function fifteen' must follow 'function fourteen'. But in more sophisticated forms of narrative than the one with which Propp was concerned there may be departures from this logical sequence; a narrator may introduce effects before their causes, as the narrators of detective stories habitually do. First the carrying off, then, as an afterthought, the eagle. This possibility, which is extremely widely used in narrative, exploiting as it does a narrator's freedom from the tyranny of real, logical sequence, introduces an important distinction in structural analysis, between the 'actual' sequence of events in a narrative and the sequence we are given to read. With most modern narratives the 'actual' sequence will have to be reconstructed, if he or she feels so inclined, by the reader; most readers no doubt follow the sequence as given without being aware of how their expectations are being manipulated.

With Propp's folktales the order in which functions occur proves remarkably constant. There is, as one would expect, no one tale which incorporates all thirty-one 'functions', but the corpus examined, of 100 tales, is a very small proportion of those which might have existed. Analysis of

Propp's kind gives the student the possibility of making up folktales of his or her own, by ordering 'functions' appropriately in patterns as yet unrealized. This is another feature of Structuralism to which I have alluded earlier: that it has, if it is successful, a certain predictive power.

The danger of a structural analysis of the kind achieved by Propp is the danger of all Formalism: that the analysis will approximate more and more to an algebra, replacing the actual constituent actions of the tales with letters of the Greek alphabet, so that all distinctions between variants are lost sight of in the search for invariants. In this respect Propp is more Formalist than Structuralist. He saw no need to try and arrange his thirty-one 'functions' in any system, by establishing oppositions between them. For this he was eventually criticized by Lévi-Strauss, who was both influenced by Propp's methods and aware of their shortcomings. He points out that if one of Propp's 'functions' can be described as 'violation of an injunction' and another as 'prohibition', these two 'functions' are surely related, the first being the contradictory of the second; just as a 'function' described as 'prohibition' is the negative transformation of another described as 'injunction'. This is the logic of transformations which Propp never grasped.

The analyses which Lévi-Strauss has made of American-Indian myths follow a similar course to Propp's analysis of folktales, but where the Formalist is content to register the distribution of 'functions', the Structuralist integrates them into a system, by opposing them one to another. Lévi-Strauss recognizes that these oppositions are much stronger in myths than they are in folktales, that where the first treat of matters that are cosmological, metaphysical or natural, the second are usually limited to the local, the social and the moral. For this reason, Lévi-Strauss suggests that folktales are an intermediate form between myth and literature, since the oppositions to be found in the latter are weaker still. His own sense of economy is such that he faults Propp for a certain profligacy in ending up with thirty-one component 'functions' when, by determining the pattern of oppositions between pairs of 'functions', the total could be reduced. The economy of his own analysis of myths, into their constituent 'mythemes', goes well beyond Propp in the Structuralist's quest for integration of his data.[11]

It is noticeable that the structural analysis of narrative as practised by both Lévi-Strauss and Propp involves certain 'descriptions' of, in the one case, 'mythemes', and, in the other, 'functions'. I have already given examples of Propp's 'descriptions', e.g. 'displacement in space between two kingdoms'. It may be that such a form of words, introduced by the analyst, would command agreement from any other analyst called on to identify functional invariants; yet it is also possible that two analysts might not agree on the characterization of a 'function' or a 'mytheme', in cases where the 'descriptions' are more subjective. There is a danger that the 'description' chosen may be loaded in the analyst's favour and stem from his desire to establish patterns of similarity or opposition. The 'descriptions' found by Lévi-Strauss in his analyses of myths have raised serious doubts as to their adequacy. In his celebrated analysis of the Oedipus story, for example, he classifies the various actions ('mythemes') according to what he asserts to be a common property. Three such 'mythemes' which fall under the one heading for Lévi-Strauss are:

1 Cadmos seeks his sister Europa, ravished by Zeus.
2 Oedipus marries his mother, Jocasta.
3 Antigone buries her brother, Polynices, despite prohibition.

The property common to these three actions, according to Lévi-Strauss, is 'the overrating of blood relations', and to them, in his analysis, there corresponds another set of actions with the opposed property in common of 'underrating blood relations'. It is far from certain that this scheme of oppositions, founded on the analyst's chosen 'descriptions' of actions in the myth, is the only one to be derived from the data. Other such schemes might be advanced by other analysts, who chose to give other 'descriptions' of the same actions.

This issue is worth raising here because it points to a crucial moment of any Structuralist analysis of literature, when it passes from the formal level of the texts it is concerned with to the semantic, or from 'form' to 'content'. The Formalists in Russia were taken to task for arguing that form came first and that content was only present in order to justify the form. Structuralism need be guilty of no such excess. It seeks, agreed, to work out a 'grammar' of literature, or set of rules which texts must exemplify either in the observance or the violation if they are to be classed as literary; and this can be achieved only by abstraction from actual texts. This is Structuralism as Poetics, set on differentiating the literary examples with which it works from a formal point of view. But there is also a Structuralism of individual texts, which seeks to analyse them structurally: that is, to relate their parts to each other and to show how this particular text 'works'.

This is not to be done without taking account of the semantic aspects of the text; on the contrary. The later Formalists themselves recognized that if a work of literature was a unity, then this unity or integrative principle was intimately connected with what the work 'meant'. Tomashevsky, for example:

> In the course of the artistic process, particular sentences combine with one another according to their meaning and realise a certain construction in which they find themselves united by an idea or a common theme. The meanings of the particular elements of the work constitute a unity which is the theme (what we talk about). We can talk equally well about the theme of the work as a whole as of the theme of its parts. Every work written in a language provided with meaning possesses a theme ... The literary work is endowed with a unity when it is constructed from a single theme which is unveiled in the course of the work.[12]

Here, again, one can see that the analysis hinges, as it does for Lévi-Strauss, on the 'description' found by the analyst for the parts of the work or even for the work as a whole. The theme is, as Tomashevsky parenthetically but crucially remarks, 'what we talk about'. The appeal here is to the 'intuition' of the reader, or that gift for textual interpretation which comes with instruction and with practice and which might better be called by Jonathan Culler's term of 'literary competence', by analogy with the grammatical 'competence' posited by Chomsky.[13] As readers we have somehow to acquire literary understanding as we once acquired linguistic understanding in order to achieve the level of readerly intuition that will lead us to a work's 'themes'. And literary understanding can reasonably be seen as structure-dependent: the structures of literature determine not *what* we understand when we read but *how* we understand it. The particular meanings we derive from our reading are the 'events', our 'competence' is the system on which those events depend. That system must be learned; there is no wholly untutored way of making sense of literature.

If there is one textual principle on which such literary understanding rests it is the principle of repetition or, as the French literary theorist A. J. Greimas prefers a little alarmingly to name it, the principle of redundancy. The notion of 'redundancy' is drawn from Information Theory, which declares as redundant whatever in a message is not new information to the person receiving it. In narrowly informational terms literature is indeed characterized by an excessive redundancy, since any literary text is marked by whole series of repetitions. If it were not so we would be quite unable to make sense of it. The 'themes' of a particular work cannot be conveyed once and never again for if they were we would fail to identify them as themes. 'Themes' involve a convergence in the mind of the reader who holds together information drawn from different parts of the text and from different moments of his reading. They involve the memory, as well as patterns of insistence in the text itself. The process, yet once more, is one of integration '. . . which enables us to orientate our understanding of

elements which are discontinuous, contiguous, hetero-
geneous (as given in the syntagm which knows of only a
single dimension, that of succession).'[14]

It is a characteristic of all literary understanding, Structuralist or not, that it works to undo the successiveness of
the text itself. The principle of linearity, dear to Saussure,
gives way to a principle of simultaneity. The thematic
repetitions we depend on in understanding may occur at
widely spaced intervals in a text, or they may occur
insistently throughout. If one takes, for example, the fundamental device in fiction of 'character', this can be built
up only repetitiously by an author, with each successive
appearance serving to *confirm* indications as to the nature,
and hence the function within the narrative, of the character in question. In semiotic terms, each item of evidence
that we are given for this purpose may be classified as an
index. Without repetition no 'character' could form in our
minds at all. (We would be incapable, that is, of 'talking
about' the character, or putting the character into our
own words.) If one substitutes the word 'character' for the
word 'myth' one can agree with Lévi-Strauss that 'The
function of repetition is to render the structure of the myth
apparent.'[15]

Where literary Structuralism is distinctive as a mode of
interpretation of texts is in taking a 'functional' view of
meaning. It asks the question: What does this or that
element of the text mean *as* an element of the (or else of *a*)
text? This is to approach the constituent parts of the text
in the same fashion as Saussure approached the signs of a
language, by discriminating between the signs' 'value' and
their 'signification'. Their 'value' is determined by the
place which they occupy within the sign-system of which
they are part; and similarly with the signs of which
literature is made. They are *literary* signs before they are
any other kind of sign, to be understood functionally in
literary terms. This was one of the key axioms laid down
by Jakobson and Juri Tynianov in the years when Formalism was evolving into Structuralism: 'The literary and

extra-literary material used in literature may be introduced into the orbit of scientific investigation only when it is considered from a functional point of view.'[16]

This might seem an unnecessary proviso until one realizes what a large proportion of textual interpretation is not literary at all, but psychological, sociological and so on. Structuralism has no business trying to suppress interpretations of these kinds, which have much to tell us about literature; but it can claim precedence over them, in so far as a structural interpretation should come first. That is to say, if we again take the example of the 'characters' in a narrative, a first interpretation of what each character 'means' should be made in terms of the place which that character is seen to occupy within the scheme of the narrative as a whole. Only in that way can we work towards the 'value' of the character. Most readers of fiction probably do this anyway; they compare the characters one with another and reach certain ethical or other conclusions about them: that they are likeable or unlikeable, good or bad, and so on. Such comparisons are made possible by our experience as readers, by our 'competence' that is, but they function within the perimeter of the structure that encloses them. Readers of *Pride and Prejudice* do not need to be enormously practised in the ways of narrative to grasp the five daughters of the Bennet family as a homogeneous group – the way is eased by the fact that they are siblings – and notable first for the differences to be observed between them. They are different from each other because they have to be, since that is what characterization entails. They form a small system within the larger system of the novel itself; it will not make sense to compare every character with every other character in a fiction, because not all of them can be thus correlated. Nothing, of course, can or will stop us relating the 'characters' we meet with in fictions to our knowledge of the period or place in which the fiction is set, our knowledge of human psychology, or our experience of flesh-and-blood people around us (we forget, the more literary among us, to what point that 'experience' involves our own descriptions of other people in terms we have picked up from our reading). But we ought to remember that in the first instance the 'characters' of a fiction belong together, as elements in that particular fiction, and that whatever evaluations we submit them to subsequently, the first evaluation is a functional one.

This same point is most trenchantly made in the very first words of a study published by Barthes of the seventeenth-century French tragedian Racine: 'There are three Mediterraneans in Racine . . .'[17] The formulation is intended to surprise if not to shock, not least because no writer might be thought to have been more indifferent to locale than Racine. But *three* Mediterraneans when the atlas tells us that there is only one sea of that name? Barthes's point is that if the Mediterranean is an element in a tragedy by Racine it is so for reasons of Racine's and not for reasons just of geography, and the moment this particular locale is inserted into a text it receives textual connotations or a textual function. We may or may not bring to it also connotations of our own, since many of us have our private 'Mediterranean' sea; those, however, are not *textual* connotations, but imports.

The connotations which it may be possible to establish for a given term such as 'Mediterranean' in a given text are not necessarily peculiar to that text, because they may be common to an author's entire *oeuvre*, or to the work of a whole generation of authors, or to a whole period of literary history. The connotations which the Mediterranean is invested with in a Racine play could as well be traditional as private ones. The important consideration is not to determine their degree of idiosyncrasy but to demonstrate, by a telling instance, the sort of instructive reading of a text or body of texts which is made possible by a Structuralist method, of correlating the very many repetitions those texts contain and integrating them into semantic units. These semantic units themselves may then be integrated into larger units still until, some Structuralists but certainly not all would say, one ends with the final integration of the whole into a single, over-arching meaning.

Structuralism, then, is aware both of the 'grammatical' aspects of literary works and of their semantic aspects: it neglects neither even if it tries, inescapably, to separate them. I see no harm in such separation, which is that between the invariant and the variable, or what is common to all comparable texts and what is peculiar to each. If we remain with 'character' as the example of a narrative device, the separation can be understood (with some difficulty) as being between what Greimas calls an *actant* and an *actor*. *Actants* are purely formal elements in a narrative, equivalent to the subject and object of a grammarian; they are parties to any action of whatever kind, personal or otherwise, but they have no names, no qualities and no meaning beyond their grammatical role. They are, in short, the product of a structural analysis, the most abstract narrative entities conceivable. *Actors*, on the other hand, are visible components of the narrative, they are the *actual* subjects and objects of the actions which occur; they may bear names and possess distinctive appearances, natures, etc. They constitute, in Chomskyan terms, the surface structure of the narrative, whereas the *actants* constitute the deep structure. Greimas can justify this division because he can show that there is no one-to-one relation between *actants* and *actors*. One 'actantial' role may be played by several actors or one 'actorial' role by several actants. Greimas's analysis, like the rather too many new terms he has invented with which to conduct it, is complicated, and I would not wish to dwell on it here, but it helps greatly to bring out the double nature of literary Structuralism as it moves on the one side towards the sort of narrative algebra by which actual narratives can be reduced to strings of symbols or a formal logic of stories, and on the other side towards an analysis of the 'themes' which are what interest most of us in any narrative. It is at the surface of the text that the two analyses meet:

126

An actor is thus the place where narrative structures and the structures of discourse, the grammatical and the semantic components, meet and are conjoined, because he is responsible simultaneously for at least one actantial and at least one thematic role which define his competence and the limits of what he does or is.[18]

In Greimas's own work the analysis of the grammatical component is far more convincing than that of the semantic component, since the urge to abstraction in him is unusually strong (witness his belief that Propp's thirty-one narrative 'functions' can actually be reduced to a single narrative 'function', a paradigmatic action from which all other actions can be derived by a logic of transformations!). For Greimas any particular narrative represents the investment of a narrative structure (a 'programme' in his parlance) by a semantic one, whereas all mere readers of narrative naturally look at things the other way round, and see the narrative structure as extractable from the semantic one. The ambition of Greimas's Structuralism is to codify the semantic aspects of narrative as thoroughly and economically as he has codified the 'grammatical'. The *actor* being the point where the two realms meet, it is from him that the semantic analysis can start. If, for example, the *actor* in a given story is a fisherman, certain semantic constraints are at once introduced which will condition the development of the narrative. Many of this actor's actions will follow from his 'thematic role' of fisherman, and so may some of the psychological characteristics with which he is endowed, fisherman being supposed by our culture to be phlegmatic, patient, etc. Greimas takes the conventional semantic view that the signified *fisherman* contains a more or less stable semantic nucleus or 'figure'. As one moves outwards from this nucleus the connotations of the term become more and more optional, even arguable. In the course of the narrative in which the 'fisherman' occurs the 'figure' will realize more and more of its potentialities, entering into relations with other 'figures' to create what Greimas calls 'figurative constellations'. Each text can be thought to constitute a semantic 'micro-universe' (Greimas rather favours astronomical metaphors) itself articulated logically from a single pair of contrary terms: an example Greimas offers is the pair of Life and Death as the fundamental logical and semantic components of the *oeuvre* of the French novelist Georges Bernanos.

A semantic analysis thus reductive, especially when it is carried out, as by Greimas, in a terminology largely imposed by himself, raises many hackles among students of literature. Greimas's Structuralism is highly elaborate and mathematical; but it is also, to the extent that one can follow his arguments, interesting and productive. If he proves to be on the right track in establishing a logic of narrative at once grammatical and semantic it will not do any harm to literature as such. It is a part of Structuralism's aim to show that works of literature are far more intricate and logical as structured than we might otherwise suspect; it is hard to see why anyone should be disturbed if this aim is made good.

A major effect of applying Structuralist principles to literary works is to enrich them semantically. Because Structuralism works by discovering correlations, and correlations between correlations, it can never treat any element of a text as if it were not at least potentially able to be correlated with some other element, of plot, or character, or whatever. In this respect Structuralism may legitimately claim to be more open-minded than other kinds of criticism, which tend to be partial in their reading of texts and to leave out of account whatever does not consort with their interests. A psychoanalytical reading of a novel may be very partial indeed, in what it chooses to interpret, and so may a Marxist reading, because both will normally seek to refer only isolated elements of the text to an extra-textual reality, rather than the text as a whole. For Structuralism everything that the text contains has to be seen as of potential consequence, which is a worrying thought, given the great length and complexity of many literary texts. Indeed, a possible argument *against* Structuralism is that if it was to be thorough it could never find time to live up to its own principles; it is a fact that much Structuralist analysis of literature has been done on relatively short or simple texts. The answer to that argument is that Structuralism, being so much less individualistic in its outlook, might very well become a collaborative form of criticism. It is unreasonable to expect a complete structural analysis of even a single text from one critic.

In theory, let us say, nothing in the text should go disregarded even if in practice it always does. The Structuralist motto, devised by Roland Barthes, is that textually and (an important qualification) to different degrees, 'everything signifies':

> This is not a question of art (on the part of the narrator), it is a question of structure: in the order of discourse what is noted is, by definition, notable: even when a detail may seem irreducibly insignificant, and alien to all function, it will still in the end mean absurdity or uselessness itself; either everything has a meaning or nothing does . . .[19]

This is equivalent to saying that everything in a text is a sign, or is connotative. Or, alternatively, that there is *something to be said* about it. The text itself might generate infinitely many other texts, which are the infinitely many readings of it made possible by the realization that it is inexhaustibly full of meanings.

The most remarkable demonstration we have yet had of what this implies is the book called *S/Z* which Barthes devoted to a novella by Balzac. (The title of the book derives, be it noted, from phonology, in which S and Z constitute separate phonemes distinguished from each other by the feature of 'voicedness': Z is voiced, S unvoiced.) The power of a text to generate commentary is shown in this case by the glaring disparity between the dimensions of Balzac's story, which are modest, and those of Barthes's analysis of it, which is considerably longer. This disproportion has been found excessive by those opposed to Barthes and to Structuralism. Rather, it is exemplary.

There is, as it happens, a scholastic exercise in France known as the *explication de texte* where such a disproportion is statutory, since it involves writing several pages of commentary on only a few lines or paragraphs of text. What Barthes has done is to transfer to the explication of prose a style of commentary more familiar and acceptable when applied to verse – a form of writing presumed to be both formally more intricate and semantically more dense. As I have earlier suggested, this is an accomplishment of Structuralism, to have caused prose to be examined with a degree of care it has seldom known before.

In *S/Z*, as in his other critical writings, Barthes is both assertive and modest. He does things to Balzac which he knows very well will be found offensive by those of other critical persuasions than his own, but at the same time seeks to deny too lasting an authority to his own methods or results. In this he looks ahead to the final chapter of this book, on post-Structuralism, in which such paradoxes will come into their own. It is a fact that the method of analysis which Barthes introduces in *S/Z* has found no disciples, which suggests a certain degree of idiosyncrasy on his part. His Structuralism is of a more personal and free-ranging kind than that of an algebraist like Greimas, but that does not mean Barthes should be excluded from a survey of Structuralism altogether. He is not rigorously or consistently Structuralist but he shows, very hearteningly, how a basically Structuralist method may be built on to by a critic of his own very high intelligence and insight.

Like any work of literature, the Balzac novella which Barthes takes as his subject – its title is *Sarrasine* – is what he calls 'plural': it is the locus of more than one meaning and hence generative of different but legitimate readings. Barthes opposes his own Structuralism to any school of critical thought which holds to the principle that a literary work has a single 'true' meaning, to discover which is definitively to 'comprehend' the work. This 'true' meaning is generally identified with the meaning intended by the author of the work, even though normally speaking the only evidence we have as readers of authorial intentions is the text itself. Much ink has been spilt in the past fifty years over the question of the 'Intentional fallacy' in literary criticism, and whether we need concern ourselves at all with an author's presumed intentions when we decide what a text's meanings are; Structuralism believes very strongly that questions of intention tend to be pointless or, at best, circular, since the evidence we use to determine them is usually drawn from the text before us.

So far as Barthes is concerned, 'intentional' readings of a text err by claiming that they are *right* and other readings necessarily either wrong or secondary:

> Some – let us say, the philologists – decree that every text is unequivocal and the bearer of a true, canonical meaning, and they dismiss second, simultaneous meanings to the oblivion of critical elucubration. Confronting these, others – let us say, the semiologists – contest the hierarchy of the denoted and the connoted; language, they say, the raw material of denotation, with its dictionary and its syntax, is one system among others; there is no reason to privilege that system.[20]

This somewhat tortuous declaration might be paraphrased as that there can be no denotative use of language in literature, if by denotation we mean a direct reference to the world outside language. If there is denotative language in literature it automatically displays itself to be so: that is, it carries a connotation of denotation because such is the function it has been allotted within the literary structure. Bakhtin, the Russian theorist of literature who comes extremely close to Barthes at many points (and was also a great 'pluralist'), makes the same argument in slightly different terms when he says that 'Reality that is unrefracted and, as it were, raw is not able to enter into the content of literature.'[21] Where Barthes writes of everything in the text being 'connotative', Bakhtin asks that we should understand it as 'ideological': it enters the text already bearing cultural values. (It was because this is the case that Bakhtin opposed the early Formalist notion of the 'resurrection' of the word as a supposedly pristine element which the author might use free from all such contamination by history or by usage.)

Operating, then, as a semiologist or semiotician of the text, Barthes invents for the purpose of analysing *Sarrasine* five 'codes' which will enable him to correlate, both grammatically and semantically, a certain number of elements of the story. He suggests that the text itself supplies him with the codes, that they are not an imposition of his own: this sly attempt to absolve himself of responsibility for the discovery and exploitation of an unusual critical method is a tribute perhaps to the austerity of a true Structuralism, which would claim to order its data by principles derivable from the data; in Barthes's case we need not take it quite seriously. Barthes is anxious, likewise, not to impose any hierarchy on the five codes, all of which are held to be equal; this too, as we shall see in a moment, is provocative.

The five codes are, briefly:

1 The 'Hermeneutic code', which groups together the various sequences of the text that first pose and then resolve 'enigmas', so creating suspense in the reader.

2 The 'Semic code', which groups together various recurrent connotations or 'themes' of the text.

3 The 'Symbolic code', the hardest to define, which groups together certain patterns of antithesis contained in the text.

4 The 'Action code', which groups sequences of actions forming self-evident wholes, however scattered they may be textually.

5 The 'Referential code', which groups all the many references made in the text to the cultural, social and other knowledge of Balzac's day.

As Barthes proceeds through Balzac's text, which he divides arbitrarily up into 'units of reading' of a few lines each, he is able to distribute these units among the 'codes'. There is no one-to-one relation between the 'units of reading' and the 'codes', because one 'unit' may be referrable to several 'codes'. Some 'units' are interpreted at length, others very briefly, as a demonstration of the necessary arbitrariness of the interpreter in deciding how far to go.

Such a reading is ingenious and very instructive, and it does lay bare levels of organization in Balzac's novella which could never otherwise have appeared. But Barthes's exercise in textual Structuralism is also biased, by the strong animus which he felt towards the ideology of Realism. Balzac is a French writer frequently chosen to exemplify nineteenth-century Realism in fiction, and thought of as a kind of social historian of his times who took his cue from what he found around him in the society of the day. He is the prime example of a writer for whom 'represenation' seems to come before 'composition' and truth to extra-textual facts before art. It is very much part of Barthes's purpose to show the error of any such naïve supposition, to show that the structures of a text like *Sarrasine* are *literary*, that it is an elaborate work of literary art, not fictionalized social observation. The demonstration is valuable, even if it goes too far. Barthes deliberately taunts those who hold to the traditional view of Realism by downplaying the importance in his scheme of the fifth, 'referential' code, which is the one Realists would set above all the others as being central to the purposes of a writer such as Balzac. They would hold that Balzac's text is full of direct and personal references to French society of the period; Barthes argues, to the contrary, that it contains no *direct* references to it at all, because it refers only to the accepted and hence impersonal wisdom of the day. That is, there is no *observation* in it, merely a large collection of second-hand opinions and beliefs. And by refusing, as he does, to establish any hierarchy among his five codes, so that the 'Referential' code gets equal weighting with, say, the 'Hermeneutic', Barthes attempts to shift the whole balance of the way in which we read a supposedly 'Realist' text towards its high degree of artifice.

What, finally, is perverse in Barthes's Structuralism in *S/Z* is that he adopts a method of analysis which serves to disintegrate Balzac's text. His refusal to subordinate any one code to the others, to make one of them the 'dominant', as the Russian Formalists would have put it, and even more his refusal to bring order to all the 'themes' uncovered by the 'Semic' code, which he prefers to leave as a scattered and seemingly random 'shimmer of meaning',[22] reveal the playful side of Barthes. The lesson he teaches is of the multiplicity of meanings and of the 'over-determination' of many elements in the text; and it is all the more effective for being taught from a text we might once have thought of as being relatively 'transparent'.

Barthes brings out explicitly the virtual endlessness of interpretation: the Peircean realization that signs can be interpreted only by the use of other signs. The limited degree of integration achieved by Barthes's 'codes' is achieved by *putting a name to* groups of elements perceived as belonging together in some way even though they are scattered in the text itself. We are used as readers to recognizing a fiction-writer's 'characters' by their proper names, which bind together their various appearances in the narrative; we are less used to the similar process by which we make sense of the narrative itself and recognize its recurrent themes. The process is one of nomination; which, Barthes tells us,

> is the very activity of the reader: to read is to struggle to name, it is to subject the sentences of the text to a semantic transformation ... reading is thus absorbed into a sort of metonymic glissade, with each synonym adding some new characteristic, some new departure to its neighbour.[23]

With many readers it is questionable whether this process ever gets explicitly under way, since there may be no call for them to 'name' anything of what they read, unless they find themselves asked to talk or to write about it. The thrust of Barthes's Structuralism is towards the inconclusive: he warns against foreclosing on the process of semiosis and the common assumption that literary texts are susceptible of only a single interpretation or directed to conveying only a single, 'final' meaning. These are warnings that connect him closely with the teachings of post-Structuralism, to which I now turn.

NOTES

1. *Readings in Russian Poetics*, ed. Matejka and Pomorska, p. 4.
2. M. Bakhtin and P. Medvedev, *The Formal Method in Literary Scholarship*, p. 84.
3. V. Erlich, *Russian Formalism*, p. 90.
4. Bakhtin and Medvedev, op. cit., p. 63.
5. F. Galan, *Historic Structures*, p. 120.
6. *Readings in Russian Poetics*, p. 85.
7. R. Jakobson, *Verbal Art, Verbal Sign, Verbal Time*, p. 51.
8. Gerard Manley Hopkins, cited in *Style in Language*, ed. Sebeok, p. 368.
9. V. Propp, *Morphologie du conte*, p. 6.
10. *Ibid.*, pp. 28–9.
11. See the essay entitled 'La Structure et la forme: Réflexions sur un ouvrage de Vladimir Propp' in Lévi-Strauss, *Anthropologie structurale Tome 2*.
12. *Théorie de la littérature*, ed. T. Todorov, p. 263.
13. See J. Culler, *Structuralist Poetics*, especially pp. 113–30.
14. R. Barthes et al., *Poétique du récit*, p. 50.
15. Lévi-Strauss, *Structural Anthropology*, p. 229.
16. *Readings in Russian Poetics*, p. 79.
17. R. Barthes, *Sur Racine*, p. 15.
18. A. J. Greimas, *Du sens 2*, p. 66.
19. Barthes, *Poétique du récit*, p. 17.
20. Barthes, *S/z*, p. 13.
21. Bakhtin and Medvedev, op. cit., p. 17.
22. Barthes, *S/z*, p. 26.
23. *Ibid.*, p. 99.

5

POST-STRUCTURALISM

In their prescient and formidable critique of the Russian Formalists (published in 1928) Bakhtin and Medvedev make the point that the Formalists' 'resurrection of the word' as a self-enclosed material entity is sterile and anti-social: 'The fear of meaning, which, with its "not here" and "not now" is able to destroy the material nature of the work and the fullness of its presence in the here and now, is the fear which determines the poetic phonetics of the formalists.'[1]

Without knowing it, and well ahead of time, Bakhtin and Medvedev here inaugurate the age of post-Structuralism. To accuse the Formalists of fear, when they so revelled in their audacity, is a clever debating-point; but it is also something more, of relevance to everyone who reads literature, and not simply myopic Formalists. Many readers *are* afraid of meaning when it threatens to distract them from the words they have in front of them. The deep insight which Bakhtin and Medvedev are here offering is into the way in which the words of a given text generate more, and different, words in our minds as we read it. Far from affording us a point of verbal stability the literary text casts us adrift in semantic space.

The argument is remarkably prophetic of those put forward more than thirty years later by the French philosopher who has created post-Structuralism almost single-handed: Jacques Derrida.[2] Derrida came to prominence in the late 1960s, when Structuralism was very much an intellectual fashion in France and had some reputable achievements behind it. He is quite certainly the weightiest and most acute critic Structuralism has had, as well as being a philosopher of power and originality. I choose here to consider Derrida as a post-Structuralist rather than by the alternative name of 'deconstructionist', by which both he and his followers have tended to be called, because the description of 'post-Structuralist' preserves within it the close relation to Structuralism on which Derrida depends for many of his effects. Post-Structuralism is not 'post' in the sense of having killed Structuralism off, it is 'post' only in the sense of coming after and of seeking to extend Structuralism in its rightful direction.

Post-Structuralism is a critique of Structuralism conducted from within: that is, it turns certain of Structuralism's arguments against itself and points to certain fundamental inconsistencies in their method which Structuralists have ignored. It takes language to be the model of a structural system more whole-heartedly even than Structuralism does, and draws unexpectedly fundamental conclusions from the way in which language works. Ultimately, Derrida's ambitions are much larger than merely to point to the weaknesses of Structuralism as commonly practised: they are to dismantle the whole system of Western thought since the time of Plato, because he believes it has been led astray by its reprehensible failure to grasp the nature of language and of meaning. In the work of Derrida the principles laid down by Saussure serve the sweeping and sceptical purpose of undermining a prevailing and generally unconscious 'idealism', which asserts that language does not create meanings but reveals them, thereby implying that meanings pre-exist their expression. This for Derrida is a nonsense. For him there can be no meaning which is not formulated: we cannot reach outside language.

The best access to Derrida's ideas for present purposes may be had by considering what he has written about Saussure, his arguments in respect of whom are typical of those he has advanced against other thinkers and writers in that they show very brilliantly where Saussure failed to grasp the full significance of his own theories. This is the speciality of Derrida's 'deconstructive' method, which brings into the open the 'blind spots' endemic in all philosophical writing if not in all creative writing (the assimilation of the two is, I am aware, dubious). The 'blind spots' are there because no one who writes is wholly master of the language which they use or of the meanings which it generates in the minds of those who read or hear it.

For Saussure the linguistic sign is differential in nature: it is what it is by virtue of what it isn't, having no value apart from that which it derives from membership of its system. Derrida accepts the truth of this axiom but extends it more widely than Saussure. With him differentiality becomes a key concept, with enormous implications for the way in which we understand both the world and ourselves. Properly understood, it contradicts what Derrida terms the 'metaphysics of presence', which he claims has dominated Western thought for more than two thousand years. The 'metaphysics of presence' presumes that whatever is present to us is wholly and immediately so, grasped in an act of pure intuition which has no recourse to signs. Presence precedes signification. If this were the case, however, it is hard to see how we could be conscious of it, since consciousness *does* have recourse to signs. Presence, according to Derrida, can never be immediate therefore, only mediated by language. We are conscious of what is present to us as *being* present; and the concept of presence, like all concepts, is not a self-enclosed unity, but one inhabited by its contrary. There can be no meaning to asserting that something is 'present' if there is no possibility of its being 'not-present': the concept of presence entails that of non-presence or absence, for such is the fundamentally differential nature of language. The presumed integrity of 'the present moment', for example, turns out to be an illusion: 'One thus very quickly realizes that the presence of the present moment can only appear as such to the extent that it is *continuously compounded* with a non-presence and a non-perception, to wit primary memory and expectation (retention and protention)'[3] (Derrida's italics).

The vocabulary here is that of Husserl, a critique of whose phenomenology Derrida is conducting. But the argument he advances cuts deep: there can be no such concept as absolute, unmediated 'presence' because as soon as we are aware of something being present to us it has entered into the circuit of signs and meanings. The notion of 'presence' acquires its value because of its opposition to the notion of 'absence', and the present is as it were contaminated by the absent: in the case of the present moment by its structural relation to the past and the future. The present moment is what it is by virtue of its membership of a temporal series.

The resort to language or signs entails, we know, the loss of all uniqueness or immediacy. The sign is not the thing itself. Derrida stresses the 'iterativity' of signs, which are by definition repeatable: 'A sign is never an event if event means an irreplaceable and irreversible empirical uniqueness. A sign which took place "only once" would not be a sign. A purely idiomatic sign would not be a sign.'[4] In the possibility of their repetition lies the identity of signs: each time it occurs we recognize a particular sign as the *same* sign as on previous occurrences. It is an 'ideal' object, not to be identified with its actual occurrences – or, in the helpful terminology of Peirce, it is the *type* of which each occurrence is a *token*.

The structure of time and of language is identical for Derrida. Any idea we might have that the 'present moment' is an absolutely simple point incapable of analysis is scotched by the patent relativism of the term 'present'. The 'present moment' is not a point but a structure, depending for its existence on its relations with past and future. Like any linguistic sign it is 'inhabited' by other signs; 'No sign is an island' we might say. Every sign contains what Derrida calls a 'trace' of signs other than itself. This is a difficult concept to catch hold of inasmuch as the 'trace' is not real, it is not 'really there'. Rather, it is a potentiality inherent in 'signhood' and the principle underlying any system of differentiation such as language. It is because of the 'trace' that we can say that one sign leads always to another, in a process of interpretation that is strictly interminable. It is thus the 'ground' of language as a system, and to be able to define it from within the language-system itself is presumably impossible. Indeed, the elusiveness of the 'trace' is a proof of its significance, since it demonstrates that signs can never be complete in themselves but refer us endlessly to other signs. (The sign *trace* itself cannot be exempted from the process.)

This process of endless referral is also termed by Derrida 'différance', a coinage of his own which forms a new French noun from the verb *différer* meaning to 'defer'. This new form is also to the French ear a homophone of the word *différence*, so that we should understand it as meaning both 'differing' and 'deferring', since for Derrida these are the same process. (The fact that *différance* and *différence* sound exactly the same in French but can be distinguished by the eye when they appear in print also has its importance: to this I shall return.) The process of referral from sign to sign need never in theory be arrested because there can be no final escape from the sign-system. Every new signified is, Derrida cruelly reminds us, also a signifier, and so on *ad infinitum*. One meets with the same reminder in the work of the American philosopher W. V. Quine, when he writes: 'What is called *giving* the meaning of an utterance is simply the uttering of a synonym, couched, ordinarily, in clearer language than the original.'[5] There is no such thing as what Derrida and Derridans choose to label the 'transcendental signified', which the idealists ask us to believe in: a meaning outside language altogether. That would be perfectly incommunicable, even to ourselves.

The inescapability of *différance* ensures that there can be no escape from time in the process of signification. Structuralism has tended to treat the systems it investigates in spatial terms, as if all the successive elements of which they are made were in fact present simultaneously. The

Saussurean emphasis on the 'coexistent' sets one free to reorder things as one requires. But such spatial or timeless models are an illusion which Derrida is eager to expose. It is fostered by the Structuralist's failure to acknowledge the temporality of his own investigations, which are successive and not simultaneous.

It is fostered also by the obvious difference between the spoken and the written forms of language, which is of central importance to Derrida. We are not likely to make the mistake of thinking spoken sequences of words to be capable of abstraction from time, because they are not preserved (if they are recorded, they no longer function as merely spoken words); it is when sequences of words are written and thus made permanent that we are easily able to think of them as somehow existing simultaneously. The text of a book – or of what we commonly call a 'volume', which is a clear enough indication of how our language transforms the temporal into the spatial – does not necessarily strike us as being extended in time, even though we know that it will take us several hours of our own time to read it, and even though, if we are Structuralists, we will not have forgotten the stress laid by Saussure on the strict linearity of all syntagma.

The 'structural reading' of a literary or other text which ignores its real extension in time carries with it for Derrida the particular danger that it will also be a teleological reading. If the text can be shown to have a structure, it is all too easy for the critic then to show that this structure is the *object* of the text and of its author. The text is thus perverted into the *realization* of a structure which pre-existed it; it is pre-determined. Up to a point many texts are pre-determined, since their authors will be writing to a plan. But only up to a point; the plan is not to be confused with the final text. Nor, above all, is the plan to be thought of as something in itself non-textual, because that is impossible. The plan too is a form of words and as such a text or structure; it can never be offered as the a-textual 'origin' of another text.

Against the pernicious idealism which promotes such illusions, Derrida pits his own strong notion of creativity. Before the text there is nothing:

> To write is to know that what is not yet produced in the letter has no other dwelling-place, is not waiting for us as a *prescription* in some *topos ouranios* or divine understanding. The meaning must wait to be said or written in order to inhabit itself and to become what, by differing from itself, it is: meaning.[6]

Derrida is arguing here against a Swiss Formalist critic, Jean Rousset, whom he accuses of emphasizing the *form* of a text to the detriment of its *force*, which is that creative energy Derrida sees to be at work in it. There are times indeed when he strikes one as decidedly Romantic, in the literary historical sense of that term, in his understanding of creativity, even though he attributes the power to create meanings to language, not to the individuals who employ it.

Derrida's wish to exorcise the 'metaphysics of presence' from our thinking has led him to concentrate his attention as a writer exclusively on the written form of language as against the spoken; indeed, he *uses* the written form to show us how we commonly misunderstand the nature of the spoken one. In this he believes, rightly, that he is countering a long-standing prejudice among those who have thought and written about language: that the written language is subordinate to the spoken, that it is the *representation* of the spoken language, itself seen as primary. If one casts an eye over the centuries of linguistic thought, one will agree that Derrida is justified in supposing that writing has been either neglected or seen as derivative. A linguist as alert and progressive as Sapir, for example, subtitles his book on *Language* 'An introduction to the study of speech', while Bloomfield, in his book also called *Language*, makes early on the remarkable statement that 'Writing is not language, but merely a way of recording language by means of visible marks'.[7]

Giving the priority to speech over writing in this way is

undoubtedly the orthodoxy in the long history of linguistic thought. It is very much to the fore in Saussure's *Course*, where the complaint is made that writing enjoys an undeserved prestige.[8] Derrida would abolish any such priority. Not, as some have imagined, because he is seeking to reverse it, and to set writing above speech as a form of language, but in order to remove it, by showing how speech and writing are both in fact forms of the one system. The traditional priority accorded to speech comes about, Derrida claims, because of the deep 'phonocentrism' of Western thought. We are sentimental towards the human voice and deluded by it into forgetting that even when we speak, or speak inwardly with ourselves, i.e. think, we still have recourse to signs. We cannot be fully 'present' even to ourselves in so far as we must of necessity commune with ourselves in a system of signs that is not ours alone but a social institution. 'Hearing ourselves speak' is the illusory model of intimacy and immediacy which Derrida suggests has enabled us conveniently to ignore the true nature of signs. It is a model which shortens the circuit of communication so much that it may no longer appear *as* a circuit:

> When I speak, not only am I conscious of being present to what I am thinking, but also of preserving in the greatest possible closeness to my thought or to the 'concept' a signifier which does not fall into the world, which I understand as soon as I utter it, which seems to depend on my pure and free spontaneity, to require the use of no instrument, no accessory, no force taken from the world.[9]

That is, the true impersonality of signs is obscured from us: we are at one with what we hear ourselves say. If this 'phonocentric' illusion is as pervasive and as tenacious as Derrida maintains that it is – it has been sustained, in part, by our reliance on a phonetic alphabet, customarily seen by linguists as an extraordinary human achievement in the phonological analysis of speech sounds – then he is faced by the problem of explaining why this should be so.

Can everyone be wrong or deluded but himself? His explanation is that such a fundamental contradiction can only be the effect of 'desire'. This is the Freudian component of Derrida's thought. We *know* that even when we commune with ourselves we cannot be fully 'present' to ourselves, but we manage to believe the opposite. This, if I follow Derrida properly, is the result of repression: we cannot face the truth of the matter, which is that we are alienated even from our selves by language. We cherish the 'phonocentric' illusion of intimacy because to acknowledge that it is an illusion is to acknowledge our own absence from the words we speak. Derrida likes to stress that the language-system, structurally understood, is a *memento mori*, because it reminds us that we may employ it but that we cannot possess it. The words which we use do not, structurally speaking, need us there in order to mean something, as we know from reading and understanding the printed words of so many dead authors. The structural nature of language, a system of constant and endless referral, also reminds us that no escape is to be got from the movement of time, that human life itself is strictly linear.

It is simpler for Derrida to make us think of signs as reminders of mortality by dealing with written language, because written signs are more self-evidently external to those who proffer them. But they are no different in this from spoken signs, which are equally external to us. Spoken and written signs are two forms of what Derrida calls 'archi-writing', the system that underlies them both. This is a system of pure differentiality: the system that Saussure failed properly to recognize because of his prejudice against writing and his residual idealism in respect of meanings. 'Archi-writing' is absolutely fundamental and all-embracing: 'This archi-writing, although its concept is called for by the themes of the "arbitrariness of the sign" and of difference, cannot and can never be recognized as the object of a science. It is what does not allow itself to be reduced to the form of *presence*.'[10] Thus 'archi-writing', 'trace' and 'différance' all function to one end in Derrida: to keep us disturbingly aware of the unstable and differential nature of signs, and of their externality or objectivity. The 'phonocentric' model of the 'hearing ourselves speak' finds its equivalent in the 'watching ourselves write'; in this instance we are less prone to fall victim to illusion because the signs we use are so very obviously 'falling into the world', as Derrida puts it, and are so very obviously 'accessory'. (The 'hearing ourselves speak' in the form of a tape-recording approximates speaking rather brutally to writing in a manner highly supportive of Derrida's thesis: it alienates us from our comfortable intimacy with ourselves.)

Derrida's own astonishing deconstructive gifts have been exercised for the most part on the texts of philosophers, for the good reason that philosophers offer arguments and are more readily open to deconstruction than writers who do not. Nevertheless, literary criticism has been much taken with Derrida's methods, and this is logical enough, because it is part and parcel of those methods not to recognize any distinction between philosophical and other kinds of writing. All, for Derrida, are inescapably metaphorical, because of the autonomy of language or, better, of the 'archi-writing'. Post-Structuralism has flourished in the literary field because literary criticism has in the past been much given to the illusion of 'phonocentrism'. We all too often assimilate what we read to what we hear. Indeed, one need only reflect for an instant on the kind of vocabulary we resort to in the discussion of written texts to appreciate the validity of Derrida's case: how often are writers not held to 'say' this or that, rather than to 'write' it; how often do we not read (or do I mean 'hear'?) of a writer writing for a particular 'audience', instead of a readership; and there are many literary critics who write of an author's 'voice' and of readers 'listening' to that voice. The critical vocabulary strays constantly towards the phonetic, as if the literary work were addressed by a speaker to a hearer, not by a writer to a reader. And this despite the fact that psychologists now assure us that we are perfectly well able to read without 'pronouncing' the words to ourselves silently as we go. 'Voice', it seems, no longer comes into it, either on the author's side or on the reader's.

This widespread but misleading view of the literary text as something 'spoken' becomes understandable when one remembers how eager we are for literature to be 'expressive'; to communicate to us, that is, the inmost thoughts and sentiments of the author in a highly individualized way. This is the lyrical view of authorship, and its corollary is that the signs which authors must use are also themselves 'expressive'. Signs have an expressive function, that is not in doubt; they are the vehicle of a certain subjectivity. But they are also 'indicative', a term which Derrida opposes to 'expressive': there is a gap which we can only struggle to bridge between what we feel and what we utter, when the first is private and ineffable and the second conventional and public. Pure expressivity is incommunicable because it lies outside the scope of our communal systems of signs:

> Everything in my discourse which is destined to manifest an experience to someone else, must pass through the mediation of the physical aspect. This irreducible mediation commits every expression to an indicative operation. The function of manifestation is an indicative function. Here we come close to the root of indication: there is indication each time the act which confers meaning, the animating intention, the living spirituality of the *vouloir-dire*, is not fully present.[11]

What Derrida asks is not that we abandon all notion that literature 'expresses' but that we temper it with a proper awareness that it must also 'indicate'. In the quotation above I have left the French term *vouloir-dire* untranslated because it brings out very neatly the disjunction on which Derrida relies between willing and saying. The disjunction is between the sayer and the said, and it is fundamental, as we have seen, to the whole Structuralist enterprise. The *vouloir-dire* model of language-use involves two moments or elements, an expressive and an indicative one, and the gap between these two moments may well be a source of extreme frustration for those who find that a system of indicative signs fails to fulfil their expressive needs.

As readers we meet with language in its indicative function, but as we read we may well hope to restore it to its expressive function: 'To reactivate writing is always to reawaken an expression in an indication, a word in the body of a letter which, as a symbol which may remain forever empty, bore within it the threat of crisis.'[12] The threatened 'crisis' is simply the chance of the text never being reactivated, of its remaining for ever unquickened by the reading process which endows it with expressivity. All texts are potentially 'dead' the moment they are written: they are inscribed and therefore capable of enduring for centuries, but this inscription cuts them loose from the circumstances of their composition and casts them adrift in the future, as indications susceptible of a great many, possibly conflicting reactivations, or of none; for, as Derrida coolly reminds us: 'In order to be what it is, all writing must be able to function in the radical absence of any empirically determined addressee in general.'[13]

An author cannot conceivably control the eventual 'reactivations' to which his or her text will become subject. That is, the meanings that are read into it may or may not coincide with the meanings which the author believes he or she has invested it with. A reasonable view is that a large number of these meanings will coincide, depending on how far separated author and reader are in time, space and culture; but that a large number of other meanings will not coincide. For language has powers of generating meanings irrespective of the wishes of those who use it. For Derrida no concept of 'mastery' is possible, by which an author may remain in control of what he or she has written (or said). The idea of a text 'communicating' meanings from author to reader is called necessarily into question:

[Writing] can no longer be understood then under the category of communication, at least if we take this in the restricted sense of the transmission of meaning. Inversely, it is in the general field of writing so defined that the effects of semantic communication may be determined as particular, secondary, inscribed and supplementary ones.[14]

Statements such as these by Derrida have been adjudged philistine, demonstrating as they do a great scepticism towards the establishment of any true channel of communication of meanings between author and reader. We are brought up as students of literature to want to *attribute* the meanings we find in it, and the only source we can ordinarily attribute them to is the author. It seems improper to attribute them to ourselves, even though it is us in whom they occur. But there is no need to attribute them to a person at all, either to the author or to the reader, since by Derrida's dispensation they may be attributed to language itself, in its indicative function. Language is quite certainly the real locus of meaning.

Thus the old anxiety about possible disparities between 'author's meaning' and 'reader's meaning' is unrealistic. A great spectrum of meanings can be got from any literary text, with certified 'author's meanings' at one end of it and blatant 'reader's meanings' at the other. In between are many meanings which could be either. Does it help to attribute them? The vitality of textual interpretation comes from disagreement, not from consensus, and the reference of meanings to the authority of a dead or absent writer is usually an attempt to eliminate disagreement by *force majeure*. If we find the uncertainty demoralizing, of not knowing on whose authority this means that, it is always possible to work to narrow the gap between 'author's meaning' and 'reader's meaning' by informing ourselves as fully as we can about the context in which the text was written – this is the end indeed to which much literary critical energy in the past has been bent. But we should not be so naïve as to imagine that we can ever close the gap; uncertainty remains.

To refer every meaning we discover in a text to its author would be absurd. To refer it, as Barthes attempts to do with Balzac's novella in *S/Z*, to five more or less conventional 'codes', is still not adequate, because what Derrida teaches us is that the text is the locus of an alarming and unstemmable process of 'dissemination'.

'Dissemination' carries further the notion relished by Barthes and by other Structuralists of the multiplicity of meanings to be found in any literary text. Even in Barthes's day this semantic hypertrophy met with angry opposition from critics who preferred to believe that canonical meanings can be agreed on for each text, and that it is not the case, when we read, that 'anything goes'. Barthes accused his opponents, the university professors, of bigotry and 'a-symbolia', meaning that they were blind to the richly connotative nature of literary language. He, and Derrida even more exuberantly after him, celebrates the knowledge that texts generate meanings with terrible liberality. There is no stopping them. The literary authorities may work to limit their number by excluding certain meanings on various grounds, as unreasonable, inconsistent, unhistorical, and so on; but these are still meanings that have arisen and that will continue to arise.

One way in particular that the meanings of a text have traditionally been kept on a leash is by the device of the summary or paraphrase. The answer to the question 'What does this passage (or text) mean?' is expected to be a good deal shorter than the passage or text itself. To give the meaning of a piece of writing is to eliminate, consciously or not, a great deal of its semantic content. Post-Structuralism, like Structuralism, contests our right to practise this sort of abridgement with a clear conscience. Derrida resists very strongly the idea that summaries can be given of a text's meaning(s), because the summaries, far from replacing or eliding particular elements in the text, actually *add* to them, being further textual elements themselves. A 'summary' is an illusion if we mistake it for the 'transcendental signified' of another text; rather, it is a text in its own right, which is why Derrida, over the years, has turned to writing about such apparently 'marginal' forms of literature as Prefaces and Introductions, in order to counter the orthodox impression of them as absolved from the iron regime of textuality. In a typical 'deconstructive' manoeuvre, he opens his book of essays called *Dissemination* with a prefatory chapter which undermines the whole notion of such prefaces, understood as encapsulating in advance what has not yet come into existence. This is a false 'essentialism'. Derrida's chapter has the ironic title in French of 'horslivre' or, literally, 'outside the book', even though it is very much inside the book. The irony is at the expense of those many of us who discriminate in essentialist terms between the 'main' and the 'subsidiary' contents of a book.

Derrida employs the notion of textual 'dissemination' to good effect against those Structuralists whom he sees as having betrayed the crucial insights of Saussure in trying to locate the 'centre' of a particular structure. Structures for Derrida have no centre, because they are structures. It can make no sense to speak of the 'centre' of a language or of any other such system. These systems are in constant 'play'. Because this is a realization unpopular with many, who crave 'centres' and 'essences', it has been 'neutralized' by a false centring of structures round a fixed point:

> This centre has as its function not only to orientate [the structure] and give it equilibrium, to organize the structure – in point of fact we cannot conceive of an unorganized structure – but to ensure above all that the organizing principle of the structure limits what we might call its *play*.[15]

A certain kind of Structuralism is here hoist with its own petard since the 'centre' which it claims to have located for its structures no longer forms part of them. From being an element among others caught within the play of relations, it is elevated above the structure to a point of privilege from where it is held to determine the play as a whole. In this way, structures as such become exempt from the rules applying to all structural activity.

Because the 'play' of signs is constant, and because the

scene of its occurrence is the mind of the readers of a text, the student of literature is placed in a new relationship to what he or she reads. Whatever thoughts we may have as readers, whether they are expressed to others or not, form a continuum with the text itself. They are, in Peirce's term, its *interpretants*, the signs evoked by the signs on the page. There are infinitely many possibilities and levels of such evocation, according to the interests, the intelligence, the knowledge, the temperament, of the reader. Readers may be arranged along a scale from the extremely passive, for whom the words of a text barely rise above the denotative, to the hyperactive, for whom they teem with connotations. Structuralism and post-Structuralism can both lead to hyperactivity in the reader, by encouraging him or her to be abnormally attentive to each moment of a text, knowing as we now do that everything in it means, and means to excess.

The role of the post-Structuralist reader is not, however, merely to register as many meanings and ambiguities as he or she can: a semantic head-count for its own sake would not do. The aim, rather, is to appreciate where and how the text under consideration falls apart, as it were: where its apparent logic and coherence can be shown to have failed, and where, in consequence, the author can be argued to have lost authority over his text. This loss occurs – indeed, is inevitable – because language has the treacherous habit of putting contradictions into texts of which their authors are unaware. The active reader comes to literature bearing in mind the proviso of the English proto-Structuralist William Empson that 'a word or grammatical structure is effective in several ways at once'.[16] This, let me stress, is a fact of literary language; we cannot, when we write, avoid a multiplicity of effects (meanings) even if we want to. The ambiguities which Empson uncovers with such extraordinary flair and delight are valid interpretations of the texts he reads, whether or not they are authorized by reference to the intentions of the writer.

The 'deconstructive' reader functions as the mouthpiece

of language, fulfilling a role already inscribed in the text under study. In the formulation of one of Derrida's most forceful and ingenious followers, Paul de Man, 'Poetry is the foreknowledge of criticism'.[17] This is provocatively put, having the form as it does of a *definition* of poetry; but all that de Man is asserting, less than outrageously, is that poetry is that knowingly ambiguous and elusive use of language *designed* for interpretation. Poets above all write in order to evoke 'texts' in those who read them. They do not want passivity in their readers. Many would not claim to be 'masters' of what they have written semantically, but to be able to offer only one perhaps of the many interpretations it is open to. Prose writers are more possessive of their meanings, but they too might admit to the justice of the post-Structuralist case, that meanings can also 'escape' them, that they should never be surprised by what others take them to have meant in writing as they have.

Post-Structuralism has deliberately exalted the role of the textual critic by denying that any real divide separates what critics do from what authors do: both write and both therefore enter into the 'play' of language and of meanings. The critic carries on from where the author leaves off, and those of us who subsequently read the critics carry on from where they leave off. The recognition of this real continuity between all who use language need not, however, stop us evaluating the contributions of its various participants differently according to what we take to be their worth. Not every author belongs above every critic merely by virtue of claiming the title of Author. The 'creative' hierarchy is not so simply drawn up as that.

The Author is a category of critical thought which both Structuralism and post-Structuralism have sought either to get rid of or, if that is too much to hope for, then to redefine in closer accordance with the facts of writing. He or she is no longer to be looked on as a fit person to be in charge of a text. The Author we are usually taught to think of as a *controlling* presence outside the text he is the author *of*. He has the power of coercing language into performing his commands, which are themselves, mysteriously, extra-textual. This is a model of external and godlike mastery of the text with which post-Structuralism especially will have nothing to do, any more than it will accept the parallel category of the Book.

All through this chapter I have adopted the post-Structuralist term, Text, to replace that of Book. Post-Structuralism deploys similar arguments against the concept of the Book as it does against that of the Author: the Book is an entity enclosed between two covers and complete in itself – a unity susceptible of an exhaustive interpretation or reducible to a manageable sum of meanings (or even a single, overall meaning). The Text, on the contrary, is not enclosed but open to the four winds of language, spawning meanings with the utmost generosity and standing in close relation to other texts. It does not have the unity of the Book, nor the singleness of purpose. And rather than being interpretable as the utterance of a single person, the Author, it is to be read as the utterance of a chorus. The text is, in Bakhtin's term for it, 'polyphonic' (Barthes goes further than that, and describes it even as a 'cacophony'); it is made up of many strands, or many 'voices' if the phonocentric model be permitted to survive. One text contains all manner of allusions to or echoes from other texts; and the many kinds of relations that can be established between one Text and others – quotation, parody, plagiarism, 'influence' – are known collectively as 'Inter-textuality'. The process of referral works in this direction too, that the signs we read may evoke in us not so much a Text of our own but other Texts of which we already have knowledge.

But if the Text has been substituted for the Book, what does post-Structuralism offer in place of the Author? The answer is the Subject who, unlike the Author, is present *in* the text rather than outside it. This is a substitution, apparently, of a flesh-and-blood person by a grammatical figure, which has caused much ill-feeling among those opposed to or uncomprehending of post-Structuralism. These Friends of the Author were not pleased – they were not meant to be – when Barthes published an essay with the title 'The Death of the Author'.[18] What is under attack in this essay, as in *S/Z* or in many other of Barthes's writings, is the common view of the Author as ultimate *explanation* of the work:

> ... the image of literature one can find in contemporary culture is tyrannically centred around the author, his person, his history, his tastes, his passions; criticism still consists for the most part in saying that Baudelaire's oeuvre is the failure of Baudelaire the man, that Van Gogh's oeuvre is his madness, and Tchaikovsky's his vice: the *explanation* of the oeuvre is always sought on the side of the man who has produced it as if, through the more or less transparent allegory of the fiction, it was always in the end the voice of one person and one person alone, the *author*, who was giving us his confidences.[19]

Barthes may have in view here a lamentably simple kind of critical thought, yet such simplicity, in respect of the relation between an Author and a Text, is all too common. Barthes, and post-Structuralism with him, would expel the Author from the Text: that is what is implied by writing of the 'death' of the Author. Authors remain, as items in literary history, with their biographies and the *oeuvre* attached to their names. But they are no longer the unified and masterful presences of old to be found at once within and without of their writing, as if they had found it possible to transfer themselves whole and without loss or distortion from life into literature. The Author is in fact a construct, or hypothesis, formed by a reader on the evidence of his or her reading. Whatever is known of an Author is textual, that is; they have no other existence for us. The process by which Authors are constructed is thus circular: we abstract them from their Texts and then use this abstraction to *explain* the Texts. The purpose of Barthes and of Derrida is to break this circle and to finally 'de-originate' the Text.

This 'de-origination' proves painful to many. We *like*

Texts to have Authors. The anonymous or collective work of literature causes anxiety, unless it is of a genre such as the ballad in which, for some reason, anonymity is held to be a virtue. We like Texts to have Authors even though many of the Authors whose Texts we read are dead, and their real 'voices' have long been silenced. We know that these dead Authors existed, but all that we have of them now are signs, not selves (unless we take selves to be constructs of signs, as we may well). These signs are far from being unequivocal or idiomatic, even though it is going too far to resolve them without remainder into quite impersonal 'codes' as Barthes does in the case of Balzac. Given the view of language on which Structuralism rests, it is quite impossible to look on the Author as some sovereign unity regulating the semantic plane of his or her writing from within. We should surely allow that to resort to language is to accept a certain surrender of selfhood in the interests of sociability.

It may be useful at this point to revert to the authorship of Structuralism's founding Text, the *Course in General Linguistics*. This, as I wrote earlier, was a Text constructed after Saussure's death by former colleagues, using the lecture-notes of those who had attended his lectures on General Linguistics. The question of how far the text as we have it represents the actual views of Saussure can never be resolved, despite extensive comparison of it with the manuscript notes Saussure left behind. We have to accept that there is a certain degree of anonymity or collaboration in the *Course* as published. Saussure's 'intentions', on which we would like to lay store, may or may not be misrepresented in it. Whatever remains of Saussure himself is textual: to wit, his other publications (very few), and the notes he left behind at his death. To compare these with the published text of the *Course* is to compare text with text; if one text contradicts the other does it necessarily follow that one is right and the other wrong? He may have changed his views in between writing the notes and delivering the lectures. And so on. We must work with the

Text we have and forget the question of its authenticity. What matters is: Are the ideas it contains good or bad, exact or inexact, fruitful or misguided? Derrida is not alone in looking on efforts to authenticate Texts by reference to some supposed ultimate authority absent from the Texts themselves as futile. They are a sign of the common nostalgia for the monolithic figure of the Author or, Derrida would say, for God, the ultimate law-giver.

To 'de-originate' the Text, then, isolates it from the inaccessible, pre-textual thoughts and projections of an Author and accentuates the effects of the act of writing itself, which are to break up the presupposed unity of the writer: 'as soon as a fact is *recounted*, for intransitive ends, and no longer in order to act directly on reality, that is to say, with no other function than the actual exercise of symbols . . . the voice loses its origin, the author enters into his own death, writing begins.'[20] The distinction which Barthes here relies on, between 'transitive' and 'intransitive' writing, is extremely close to, if not identical with the old Formalist distinction between a literary and a non-literary use of language. If we write 'transitively', with a view to achieving certain precise and practical ends by what we write, the presumption is that we retain a certain authority over what we write; we aspire to and usually achieve unambiguous messages. But when we write 'intransitively' the writing becomes an end in itself; we submit more or less willingly to the dynamic and ambiguating energies of language itself. Barthes is extending, with a slightly new terminology, a model of the relations conjoining writer and language which in France dates back to the poet Mallarmé in the second half of the last century. Mallarmé it was who wrote of the poet's role being to 'cede the initiative to words'.

Far from consolidating the Author as a presence, writing, in Barthes's very influential use of that word, undoes him: he is disseminated, as Balzac is disseminated in *S/Z*. The Subject is present in the Text in a great many dispersed fragments, a presence among other presences and without any hold over them. The Subject can only achieve a limited reintegration by the efforts of the reader, who is free to work against the disseminating force of the Text and construct some kind of coherent Figure who can be classed among the Text's 'themes'. If the word Author were not taboo we might eventually hope to recycle it, to apply to the textual Figure we have constructed from the perceived insistences and idiosyncrasies we have identified, rightly or wrongly, in reading. But if we call this Figure the writer, and retain the term Author for the real person who exists or who once existed outside the Text, we can say that writer and Author are not one but two. We cannot legitimately argue from the characteristics we believe we have established for the writer to the characteristics of the Author; we speak glibly of Authors 'putting themselves into their books' without allowing for the obscure and problematical relation which that phrase epitomizes.

It might be assumed that we practise the reintegration of scattered Authors with the greatest justification when the Subject of the Text appears in it in the first person, as in most autobiography (there are rare examples of autobiography being written in the third person). But the first person enjoys no peculiar privileges in this regard: it is still a linguistic sign and not exempt from the conditions of signhood. It does not, that is, embody a 'presence' denied to other signs, even though we may lazily assume in reading first-person texts that it does. Just as there are explicitly autobiographical writings written in the third person, so there are explicitly fictive writings written in the first. Derrida argues tellingly against Husserl that he contradicts himself by claiming that the pronoun 'I' means something new each time it is used by someone different. As Derrida observes, we understand the first-person pronoun even though we know nothing of the person using it and even though the person using it, as in a literary Text, may be long dead: 'And just as the value of a statement of perception did not depend on the actuality or even the possibility of perception, so the signifying value of "I" does not depend on the life of the speaking subject ... My death is structurally necessary to the uttering of "I".'[21]

The nature of the linguistic sign being what it is, the first-person 'I' negates the possibility of any 'self-presence' of whoever uses it: 'I' is the conventional representation of the Subject, nothing more. When Derrida writes: 'My death is structurally necessary to the uttering of "I"', he is pointing yet again to the implication of all signs, that they do not need us there to sustain them. The 'I' which I write here and now is as present to me as it ever can be but it is no sooner written than it starts to recede into the past; it may of course outlive me but never achieve any subsequent reanimation in the mind of a compassionate reader. Derrida offers much for our discomfort in the rigour of his argument against the 'metaphysics of presence'.

It follows from all that has been said (i.e. written) in this chapter that post-Structuralism is dismissive of the notion of Truth in the interpretation of Texts. It is so because of the exclusiveness which inevitably attends on that notion. If a critic claims to have discovered the 'truth' of a Text, interpretations other than his own must be presumed to be untrue and thereby disqualified. Structuralism and post-Structuralism are libertarian in this respect, that they assert the inexhaustibility of the Text and thus its perpetual openness to new critical discoveries. The Truth is an unwanted 'theological' concept, out of place in the study of literature or, Derrida would certainly add, any other kind of writing. Once revealed, it brings the process of interpretation to a stop, such is its prestige. Worse still, where Derrida is concerned, the Truth is regularly looked on as something waiting 'within' the Text to be uncovered. This is a metaphorical and a spatial usage that is anathema to Derrida, for whom Texts have no 'within' or 'without' because they exist entirely as a surface, extended in time. The so-called Truth is a part of the critic's own Text or discourse, and as a signified no more transcendental than any other. The idea of the interpreter's task as being to 'unveil' hidden Truths in this fashion is one which Derrida has attacked with zest, especially in its psychoanalytical version. He is extremely sharp with Jacques Lacan, who was unwise enough to draw a distinction between 'empty speech' and 'full speech' according to whether a patient's words to his analyst were truly 'meant' or not: it is the analyst's job to turn 'empty speech' into 'full speech' by getting the patient to acknowledge and thus to take responsibility for his words. 'Full speech' is, or should be, therapeutic.[22] But by what criterion is its 'truth' to be decided if both sequences of signs are identical? Lacan's distinction depends on the – to Derrida – untenable view that a speaker may be intimately identified with his or her words. 'Full speech' betrays a mystical or intuitive attitude incompatible with the use of signs. All speech must be classed as 'empty'.

Derrida does not claim that his own words accede to a Truth denied to the words of others. On the contrary. He accepts the conditions of language, and its metaphorical nature. Deconstructive interpretations offer no lasting truths but rather further texts which, were we so inclined, we might attend to ourselves in deconstructive vein. As readers we must dwell in what Paul de Man calls a 'state of suspended ignorance' or of what others call 'undecidability'. Post-Structuralism differs from Structuralism in being a philosophy of Becoming rather than of Being: it is endlessly dynamic, allowing us no escape or apparent respite from the shifting play of meanings. It is systematic in demanding the collaboration of others in its critical tasks, because of its axiom that all literary or philosophical texts contain within them contradictions or 'blind spots', which it is the responsibility of their successor texts to elucidate. Derrida would make philosophers of us all in so specifying the critical task:

> The reading must always aim at a certain relation, unperceived
> by the writer, between what he controls and what he does not
> control in the schemata of the language he is using. This
> relation is not a certain quantitative apportioning of shadow

and of light, weakness or strength, but a signifying structure that the critical reading must *produce*.[23] (Derrida's italics)

This singling out of a Text's 'blind' moments, where the Author has lost control of his argument, is carried a long way by those literary critics who follow Derrida. They would probably all of them enthusiastically endorse the Freudian view that such 'blindness' is a symptom of some deep 'desire' which the Author has failed to acknowledge to himself. By this sort of deconstructive reading, the Text may come to seem like the revenge of language on authorial presumption, and the deconstructive critic to be the agent of that revenge, since it is in his or her subsequent Text that blindness becomes sight. This is an aggressive role to play, and it is noticeable that the subtler post-Structuralists take trouble to defend themselves against accusations that rather than operating as critics of Texts they are using Texts to score off Authors. Their defence is to invite us, as their readers, to read their own writings deconstructively. Thus Paul de Man asks us to accept that 'Critics' moments of greatest blindness with regard to their own assumptions are also the moments at which they achieve their greatest insight.'[24] They do provided we, the critics' readers, are clever enough to see where it is they have gone wrong. De Man's paradox, whereby critical misapprehension turns out to be the highest form of apprehension, has the effect of making misapprehension seem deliberate on the part of the critic, as if he or she were appealing for our help. Blindness so productive seems like a blindness willed. The Derridan defence against such a charge, however, would be that will does not come into it, where Texts are concerned, since the necessary work of confusion and misapprehension will be done by language, in all its glorious autonomy.

Post-Structuralism, even more than Structuralism, might be accused of idolizing language, or of behaving towards it as animists behave towards the natural world. It can easily exaggerate the undoubted power of language to develop its own impetus and to go its own way, irrespective of whatever intentions we have brought to it or whatever control we fancy we have exercised over it when we reread what we have written. The weakest point in the post-Structuralist argument occurs when that argument is turned against post-Structuralism. Do we believe deconstructionists when they assure us that they are ready and even hoping for their own Texts to be deconstructed? Do we have the intelligence, or the time, or the patience so to read them? And if we do not, and the deconstructionists know that we do not, are they not then open to the charge that they are tricking us, by declaring from positions of authority that they have no authority? Post-Structuralism pretends to an abdication from power and responsibility which it knows is impossible and might even admit in a candid moment is undesirable. Its libertarian assertions of the autonomy of the Text are authoritatively made, and by authors.

This contradiction is in fact explored with humour and with a wry honesty by Barthes in his inaugural lecture at the Collège de France. In the course of it he playfully asserts his own diffidence and 'marginality' as an interpreter of literature to an audience he knows to have been invited to listen to him, on the contrary, as a central and renowned authority.[25] Without irony, which is a strong feature of post-Structuralism, such a position would seem deceitful.

Post-Structuralism may be seen as having gone beyond (or as having 'deconstructed') the binary obsession of much Structuralism, especially as formulated by Jakobson and Lévi-Strauss. The kinds of opposition of terms on which Jakobson's distinctive-feature analysis in phonology, or Lévi-Strauss's readings of myth, depend, are too stark for Derrida, who searches, as it were, 'beneath' or 'between' them in order to show the falsity of opposing them. 'Betweenness' is a key concept in Derrida for, as he writes, 'The word "between" has no full sense in itself.'[26] It is a word or sign which leads the mind instantly on because it is so obviously incomplete: it *calls for* completion and so exemplifies very neatly Derrida's entire case for the productivity of language.

Opposed terms he distrusts, therefore, as having been endowed with a spurious completeness in themselves. There is no place in his philosophy for any such final-seeming disjunctions. His own philosophical method leads him to dissolve oppositions and restore the terms to the continuity of language from which they may appear to have been torn. The fundamental opposition against which he has campaigned, as we have seen, is that between 'presence' and 'absence'. This is an opposition which occurs prominently in Saussure, who takes it to underlie his linguistic opposition between the syntagmatic and paradigmatic axes of language: the first being language as 'presence', the second language as 'absence'. Given the utter interdependence of these two aspects of language, it is surely right for Derrida to want to get rid of the notion that presence and absence are somehow irremediably opposed to one another; here too, he may be said to be correcting Saussurean Structuralism for its own good in accordance with the arguments of Saussure himself. What Derrida seeks, in this instance as in others, is not to turn the traditional hierarchy upside down, so that we take absence to be the higher term and presence the lower, but to make us see both terms as bearing the 'trace' of the other so that our minds can find no resting-place in either extreme.

And so with other supposedly fundamental oppositions, all of which fail to take account of the principle of *différance*. Indeed, we cherish them, it seems, for this very reason, that they *deny* that principle and so afford us comfort, against the realization of our own mortality and dependence. Thus Derrida takes the old metaphorical opposition freely resorted to by philosophers and others between the 'spirit' and the 'letter' of textual meanings and relates it to the age-old opposition between 'body' and 'soul'. But where most would assume that the semantic opposition between letter and spirit derived metaphorically from the more basic opposition of body and soul, Derrida argues the other way round: 'The opposition between body and soul is not only at the centre of this doctrine of meaning, it is confirmed by it; as it has basically always done in philosophy, it depends on an interpretation of language.'[27] So that, according to Derrida, the very conception of the human soul, as a spiritual 'essence' not to be identified with the phenomenal body of the person, comes about through the prevalent Western misunderstanding about language. The 'soul' would be a transcendent entity, complete in itself, exempt from the ceaseless and ultimately mortal play of signs. It has therefore to be disqualified; the 'soul', just like 'God' or any other presumedly transcendental signified, turned out to be just one more signifier, not outside the play of signs but within it. Derrida himself takes pleasure in thus stopping up what have long been seen as avenues of escape from the 'prison-house of language'.[28] For all the irony which he displays, and his admissions of scepticism even in respect of his own arguments, there is a coerciveness in Derrida's writings; and the thinker's traditional will to authority.

As a thinker he has carried the insights of Structuralism as far perhaps as they can go, and given to the thought of Saussure's *Course* a coherence which it lacked, even though it took Derrida to reveal that lack. Post-Structuralism may reasonably be looked on as the completion of Structuralism: in its own terms, as the 'insight' which Structuralism was calling for in its 'blindness'. Post-Structuralism has also carried further the project of Structuralism to show us how far we are free and how far constrained as users of signs. Structuralism allows us the considerable freedom to organize our acts of *parole* as we wish, respecting only the rules of the language we are using; it leaves us still in command of what we say or write though conscious that every sign that we employ is socially, not personally authorized. Post-Structuralism argues that any such 'command' is an illusion, that once we enter language, as speaking or writing subjects, we are as subservient to it as it is to us.

There is no knowing which is on top at any given

moment of a Text. Derrida tells us we are wrong to want to know. Another opposition which he thus discards is that between the voluntary and involuntary uses of language, which he scornfully describes as 'a very coarse tool when it comes to treating of the relation to language'.[29] Coarse or not, it is a tool we are accustomed to wielding, especially since Freud. In pre-Freudian times, there were no doubt many readers and critics of Texts who assumed that everything in them was voluntary, that the Author's will was paramount at all times. Then, however, we began to learn of 'unconscious' meanings, smuggled into the Text by desires the Author could not or would not acknowledge. These, we triumphantly decided, were what the Author 'really' meant; the conscious will could not compete with the unconscious when it came to revelations. Gratified as we feel to uncover textual meanings hidden as we suppose from their Author, we may be reluctant to abandon this Freudian model. Derrida argues that we should, by refusing to recognize any distinction at all between willed and unwilled or 'unconsciously' willed meanings. An Author must will, or there can be no Text, but we have no sure way of telling *what* he has willed.

Post-Structuralism serves to correct our view of writing and of authorship and to make it more realistic. To read literature in the light of Derrida or Barthes is to read it in a frame of mind closer to that in which it is written. The influence which language exercises over our minds when we resort to it does not have to be a guilty secret. When we use it 'intransitively', for some literary purpose, we are as likely to feel that it has failed or disappointed us as that it has served us fully; and we know, without perhaps being as morbid about it as Derrida would like us to be, that in the resort to signs we abandon the possibility of an entire subjectivity. That does not stop us enjoying language nor renewing the struggle to try and get it to do what we want. The fluency and extent of Derrida's own writings are one proof that there is nothing in the doctrine of post-Structuralism which need cause us to fall pessimistically silent.

NOTES

1. M. Bakhtin and P. Medvedev, *The Formal Method in Literary Scholarship*, p. 105.
2. It is possible that the translator of this passage from the Russian, working in the late 1970s, was influenced in his choice of English terms by the idiom of post-Structuralism; so that the 'Derridan' pre-echoes have been accentuated. Nevertheless, the closeness in thought between Bakhtin/Medvedev and Derrida is striking.
3. J. Derrida, *La Voix et le phénomène*, p. 72.
4. *Ibid.*, p. 55.
5. W. V. Quine, *From a Logical Point of View*, p. 11.
6. Derrida, *L'Ecriture et la différence*, pp. 21–2.
7. Bloomfield, *Language*, p. 21.
8. Saussure, *Course in General Linguistics*, pp. 24–31.
9. Derrida, *Positions*, pp. 32–3.
10. Derrida, *De la Grammatologie*, p. 83.
11. Derrida, *La Voix et le phénomène*, p. 41.
12. *Ibid.*, p. 91.
13. Derrida, *Marges de la philosophie*, p. 375.
14. *Ibid.*, p. 369.
15. Derrida, *L'Ecriture et la différence*, p. 409.
16. W. Empson, *Seven Types of Ambiguity*, p. 2.
17. P. de Man, *Blindness and Insight*, p. 31.
18. Barthes, *Le Bruissement de la langue*, pp. 61–9.
19. *Ibid.*, p. 62.
20. *Ibid.*, p. 61.
21. Derrida, *La Voix et le phénomène*, p. 108.
22. Derrida, *Positions*, p. 113.
23. Derrida, *De la Grammatologie*, p. 227.
24. P. de Man, op. cit., p. 109.
25. Barthes, *Leçon*.
26. Derrida, *La Dissémination*, p. 250.
27. Derrida, *La Voix et le phénomène*, p. 37.
28. This is the title of a book by the American Marxist literary critic Frederic Jameson, which takes issue with the excessive formalism, as Jameson sees it, of all Structuralism, and its corresponding disengagement from the realities of history.
29. Derrida, *La Dissémination*, p. 109.

CONCLUSION

Derrida has not yet, mercifully, written a Conclusion for any of his books which demolishes the whole purpose and practice of writing conclusions. They are, of course, very un-Derridan. By summarizing certain of the arguments which have been advanced earlier in the text they attempt to limit the 'play' of signification. Particular meanings which the Author – who is now constituted, since his Text is complete – wishes to reinforce get repeated, and the reader's mind is recalled to order.

In my own Conclusion I shall compromise. Rather than add a retrospective and semantically constrictive summary I will take up a matter alluded to but not developed earlier in the book: of the relation between system and system-user as Structuralism poses it. A great deal of the contention with which Structuralism has been surrounded turns, I suspect, on how it sees and presents this relation. For Structuralism is bound to play down the role of the individual agent in the fields of inquiry it opens up. It runs counter to the ideology of individualism in which most of us are brought up in our society. We learn to exalt the influence and originality of the individual at the expense of those systems and institutions within which individuals must function. By turning our attention to the systems and institutions Structuralism restores a balance that has often been lost. It makes it harder for us to see the individual agent as a superior element, exercising an untoward power over an economic, social, political, literary or any other system. The agent is within the system and must function by its rules. We recognize this happily enough when the system in question is an economic one, because of the obvious dominance of economic structures over economic agents; but we recognize it rather less in, say, our political, administrative or cultural life, where the scope of the individual is extremely limited in fact but grossly inflated in the popular imagination.

The question is how far Structuralism should go in its drive against the ideology of individualism; how much room should it leave for our freedom as individuals to operate within a system of constraints? There is no doubt but that the text of Saussure's *Course*, as we have it, introduces a bias into Structuralism, because it concerns itself almost exclusively with the *langue* at the expense of *parole*. This is to ignore the role of the individual speaker or writer who makes concrete use of the language-system. The predominance which Saussure accords to *langue* is one consequence of his practising a linguistics of the word, for it is at the level of the word that we have, as users of language, the least freedom. New words do get created and some of them are eventually received into the language, but generally we must all of us submit absolutely to the lexicon of our native language as it is given to us. It is at the level of the sentence that our freedom in the use of language starts to take effect. We are free to combine words in syntagma which may well be unprecedented. And at higher levels than the sentence – at the level of the literary Text – our freedom is even greater; many sentences used in isolation every day may well come from stock, but no Text comes from stock, it is sure to be different in very many respects from any Text pre-existing it. A linguistics of the sentence has a better chance of bringing out this freedom – it is of the essence for Chomsky – than the Saussurean linguistics of the word.

The same imbalance, towards *langue* and away from *parole*, is reinforced in Structuralism by its having to do with written language. Written language is – *pace* Derrida – different from spoken in being unable to register much of the 'individuality' we are able to give our spoken utterances by the use of intonation, cadence, pitch alterations, and the like. These devices 'individualize' our sentences, though it is vital to remember that they are themselves institutional and not personal. Bakhtin, who was critical of Saussure's neglect of *parole*, but equally critical of any idea that actual utterances in a language lay outside the purview of linguistics altogether, as being unique events, took 'intonation' to be of prime importance for Structuralism: 'In intonation, discourse enters into immediate contact with life. And it is in intonation first of all that the speaker enters into contact with his listeners: intonation is eminently social.'[1] Bakhtin would thus redirect the attention of structural linguists towards the very complex and far-reaching structure of *dialogue*, so reminding Structuralism of its vocation as a profoundly social method of inquiry.

In writing, that degree of freedom from the stipulations of *langue* which in speaking we achieve by means of such devices as intonation comes by the achievement of what is traditionally known as a 'style'. Style in writing, we can agree, is a fact, provable these days by computerized word and word-class counts of a particular writer's *oeuvre*. But the fact of style in no way contradicts the Structuralist view of language (or of literature); indeed, it confirms it. A style is the sum total of those particularities of language-use by which one writer may be distinguished from others. If there were only one writer writing in a language, he could not be said to have a style. Style is difference, either from others or from what are recognized as the 'norms' of language-use in a given period in a given literature (or other cultural practice). Style is internal to language: 'Style is not an absolute, a something that is to be imposed on the language . . . but merely the language itself, running in its natural grooves, and with enough of an individual accent to allow the artist's personality to be felt as a presence, not as an acrobat.'[2] Sapir's 'individual accent' strikes the only balance possible between system and agent. In Saussurean terms, it is an 'event'. The 'event' is *produced* from the system, and is comprehensible for that reason. In the words of another American anthropologist, Marshall Sahlins: 'An event is not just a happening in the world; it is a *relation* between a certain happening and a given symbolic system.'[3]

Structuralism does not seek to abolish individuality, only to define it accurately. Individuality can only be a relation, not something absolute. It is a differential and, in the case of human individuality, therefore a social concept. It is the existence of others which affords us the possibility of individualizing ourselves. Structuralism lays stress on what is common to all individuals within a given system, to all users of a language let us say; but it does not claim that its models of the system prescribe down to the last detail what events will occur within it. That would be absurd. Indeed, one might argue that Structuralism brings out with a new clarity the *distinction* between constraint and freedom, or what belongs to the system and what is specific to the actual 'event'.

Given which, it may seem puzzling that Structuralism should have acquired such a bad name, for attempting to eliminate subjectivity altogether. If it has so, this is attributable to a bias powerfully evident in the thought of certain French Structuralists. The Subject does not emerge unscathed from the work of Barthes and Derrida, as we have just seen. But they appear quite mild in their anti-subjectivism compared with Claude Lévi-Strauss, for whom Structuralism is something like an objectivist creed. As such, his views raise the important and perplexing question of 'where' structures should be located: in the 'real' or external world, or in the mind which observes and cognizes that world?

'Structure itself is a primordial fact', Lévi-Strauss asserts, and thereby reduces the role of the observer to a subordinate one.[4] There would be structures in Nature, it seems, even if there were no human beings on earth to discover and to formalize them. This is an extreme position, but Lévi-Strauss has never concealed the disgust he feels at what for him are the excesses of human self-centredness, and his corresponding admiration for the impersonality of 'hard' science. It is his hope that Structuralism may cleanse the human sciences of introspection masquerading as observation: 'What structuralism tries to accomplish in the wake of Rousseau, Marx, Durkheim, Saussure and Freud, is to reveal to consciousness *an object other than itself*; and therefore to put it in the same position with regard to human phenomena as that of the natural and physical sciences'[5] (Lévi-Strauss's italics). A Structuralist explanation of why Lévi-Strauss is capable at times of such virulence in his defence of objectivity would be to locate him within the 'system' of French philosophical thought of his time. It then becomes clear what a lasting animus he feels against post-war Existentialism, with its overblown cult of the 'free', strong-willed individual who goes through life creating his own values by his acts. Existentialism was a philosophy of freedom and human autonomy; Structuralism, and especially Lévi-Straussian Structuralism, is a philosophy of self-effacement and constraint. Lévi-Strauss *opposes* his ideas to those of Existentialism and in particular to those of Existentialism's most colourful and venerated proponent, Jean-Paul Sartre.

But Lévi-Strauss's antagonism to Sartre and all his works should not lead us tamely to discount his anti-subjectivism as a personal quirk, as the 'style' by which he has distinguished himself; there is a more substantial issue than that. In his function as writer – that is, as analyst of the systems of kinship, or ritual, or myth, with which he is engaged – he claims no subjective privileges whatsoever. The structures are *there* and so eager, it would seem, to reveal themselves, that the analyst need account himself nothing more than 'the insubstantial place or space where anonymous thought can develop, stand back from itself, find out and fulfil its true tendencies and organization, while coming to terms with the constraints inherent in its very nature.'[6] This is a remarkable statement of abdication before the evidence, though reminiscent of Roland Barthes's similar moment of abdication before his audience at

the Collège de France. Lévi-Strauss's ambition for himself
is simply to realize certain virtualities of a logical system
fully if mysteriously capable of functioning without him.
The conception is one which he refers to as a 'concrete
logic': meaning a logic of the data themselves which may be
determined merely by their rearrangement. This 'concrete'
logic is opposed to the 'theoretical' kind which is imposed
on the data from outside and arranges them in accordance
with some preordained and extraneous schema. Structuralism, as Lévi-Strauss proposes it, does not *add* to its data:

> Contrary to formalism, structuralism refuses to oppose the
> concrete to the abstract, and to accord the second a privileged
> value. *Form* is defined in opposition to a matter that is foreign
> to it; but *structure* has no distinct content; it is the content
> itself, apprehended in a logical organization conceived of as a
> property of the real.[7]

Self-effacement can go no further. Lévi-Strauss does not
carry many with him, however, in arguing that the logic
of culture which his Structuralism reveals contains that
Structuralism itself. To make such a claim entails taking
up a godlike position somewhere outside the logical system,
which is impossible. Lévi-Strauss's anonymity is a cloak
rather than a feature of his own system of thought.

Yet, in so belittling his role, Lévi-Strauss, like Barthes at
his inaugural lecture, does so from a position of great
authority.[8] He knows very well the position within the
discipline of social anthropology which his writings and
teachings have earned for him. His humility must appear
extremely forced. If the 'logic' of the concrete is in fact
capable of such simple explication, on its own terms, it is
surprising we have had to wait so long for it to find its
chosen spokesman, Claude Lévi-Strauss. It is possible
to sympathize with his distaste for subjectivism and the
distortions it leads to in our evaluations of intellectual
endeavour and achievement, without following him all the
way to the complete abolition of the subject. This is a
biased Structuralism, used in the service of a local polemic.

By so firmly projecting his structures outside himself, however, Lévi-Strauss is offering a possible solution to what the far more careful and conciliatory Piaget describes as 'the central problem of all structuralism': 'have composite wholes always been composed, but how or by whom, or were they first (and are they still) in the process of composition?'[9] In other words: are structures already there ('pre-formed' is Piaget's term for them) or are they made, by us? The conception of a structure as a closed, autonomous whole tends, as Piaget observes, to the belief that it must be pre-formed: hence 'the perpetual renascence of platonic tendencies in logic or mathematics, and the success of a certain static structuralism among those fond of absolute beginnings or positions independent of history and psychology.'[10]

Piaget faces up to the problem which exercised Husserl so greatly: which is how the individual comes to comprehend and 'internalize' the objective structures of logic and mathematics. These we adjudge to be necessary, *a priori*; they are universally valid. But children do not immediately recognize them, they must *learn* them: a process which, according to Piaget, may take up to twelve years. Hence it is the *acquisition* of structures that becomes the interesting question, rather than any naïve attempt to locate them either in the world or in the mind. Piaget proposes a middle way of 'constructivism' or, more elusively, of an 'operational structuralism', to account for the fact that we do, for example, come slowly to an understanding of the structures of mathematics. In Piaget's model, the 'necessity' or universality of these structures is not a datum for the individual but an achievement: the end-product of a process of structural learning and adaptation inscribed in the organism.

Structuralism should in fact serve to undo the old dichotomy between subject and object. The structures it 'discovers' are 'between' and not to be attributed to either pole of an illicit disjunction between the mind and the world outside it. Lévi-Strauss may rely on schemes of paired oppositions in his analysis of culture, and thus appear to make intelligibility depend on division, but he is also the man who reminds us, simply enough, of an even more fundamental unity, in the acknowledgement that 'the mind is able to understand the world only because the mind is itself part and product of this world'.[11]

NOTES

1. Quoted in T. Todorov, *Mikhail Bakhtin: The Dialogical Principle*, p. 46.
2. Sapir, *Language*, p. 226.
3. M. Sahlins, *Islands of History*, p. 153.
4. Lévi-Strauss, *The Naked Man*, p. 627.
5. *Ibid.*, p. 629.
6. *Ibid.*, p. 625.
7. Lévi-Strauss, *L'Anthropologie structurale Tome 2*, p. 139.
8. For a further example of this same tactic, see M. Foucault, *L'Ordre du discours*, where, also in an inaugural lecture at the Collège de France, Foucault begins: 'Rather than give utterance [*prendre la parole*], I would have liked to have been enveloped by it ... instead of being the one from whom discourse comes, I would rather have been at the mercy of its unfolding ...' (pp. 7–8).
9. J. Piaget, *Le Structuralisme*, p. 10.
10. *Ibid.*, p. 53.
11. Lévi-Strauss, *The View from Afar*, p. 118.

BIBLIOGRAPHY

In the bibliography which follows I give details only of books, not of scattered articles. The total number of publications on Structuralism in the past twenty years or more has been enormous; the items mentioned here are those I have myself found valuable and which seem to me to form the core of a reading list. In the many instances where the books concerned were written in French or other languages I have provided first the title of the English translation (if any) and then that of the original.

A. GENERAL

There are surprisingly few general books on Structuralism. The most comprehensive and rigorous is that by the eminent Swiss psychologist Jean Piaget: *Structuralism* (*Le Structuralisme*, 1968. Trans. Chaninah Maschler. London: Routledge and Kegan Paul, 1971). This is angled very much towards mathematics and the sciences, and is far from elementary. The only other attempt by a single author worth signalling is Terence Hawkes's *Structuralism and Semiotics* (London: Methuen, 1977), which ranges widely, is angled much more towards literary Structuralism and is elegantly written. Among collective volumes, an early example is *Structuralism* (ed. J. Ehrmann. New York: Doubleday Anchor, 1971); this was originally a special issue of the journal *Yale French Studies* (Nos 36/37, 1966), and contains articles both by leading Structuralists (Claude Lévi-Strauss, Jacques Lacan, A. J. Greimas, etc.) and on Structuralism by academics; as a whole the book is rather advanced. Simpler are the essays contained in *Structuralism: An Introduction* (ed. David Robey. Oxford: Clarendon Press, 1973), which contains seven lectures given in Oxford by prominent specialists. *The Languages of Criticism and the Sciences of Man* (ed. Richard Macksey and Eugenio Donato. Baltimore: Johns Hopkins University Press, 1970) contains the proceedings of a conference held in 1966, with contributions both for and against Structuralism by, among others, Roland Barthes, Jacques Derrida and Tzvetan Todorov. Of a different kind is *Structuralism and Since* (ed. John Sturrock. Oxford: OUP, 1980), which consists of five essays by specialists on the work of Lévi-Strauss, Barthes, Michel Foucault, Lacan and Derrida. Finally, a useful anthology of Structuralism in action in various fields is *Structuralism: A Reader* (ed. Michael Lane. London: Jonathan Cape, 1970).

Of the French books that have not been translated, or not fully translated, the weightiest, though quite advanced, is *Qu'est-ce que le structuralisme?* (ed. François Wahl. Paris: Seuil, 1968), which contains five substantial essays on Structuralism in linguistics, literature, anthropology, psychoanalysis and philosophy. There is also a smaller, brisk survey, more on the social sciences than on literature, in Jean-Marie Auzias, *Clefs pour le structuralisme* (Paris: Seghers, 1971).

B. LANGUAGE

The absolutely key text is Ferdinand de Saussure's (1857–1913) *Course in General Linguistics* (*Cours de linguistique générale*, 1916. Trans. Roy Harris. London: Duckworth, 1983). This expert translation replaces, for me, the earlier English version, by Wade Baskin, which is still available. There is a magnificently annotated edition of the *Cours* in French, by Tullio de Mauro (Paris: Payot, 1974), which provides a great deal of information on Saussure and discussion of his ideas. For an excellent short study of his doctrines in English there is a 'Modern Master' volume,

Jonathan Culler's *Saussure* (London: Fontana, 1976). Of nineteenth-century works in linguistics to some extent prophetic of Saussure and of Structuralism, two that stand out are Wilhelm von Humboldt's *Linguistic Variability and Intellectual Development* (*Uber die Verschiedenheit des menschlichen Sprachbaues*, 1836. Trans. G. C. Buck and F. A. Raven. Coral Gables: University of Florida Press, 1971) and the American W. D. Whitney's *The Life and Growth of Language: An Outline of Linguistic Science* (New York: Scribner, 1875).

The North American tradition of linguistic Structuralism is ideally exemplified in the short book by Edward Sapir (1884–1939), *Language: An Introduction to the Science of Speech* (the most recent edition of which is London: Hart-Davis, 1971). *Edward Sapir: Appraisals of His Life and Work* (ed. Konrad Koerner. Amsterdam and Philadelphia: John Benjamins, 1984) is valuable for reprinting the long and most informative review of Sapir's work by the American structural linguist Zellig S. Harris (1949). The other classic text of North American Structuralism is Leonard Bloomfield's (1881–1949) *Language* (first published in Britain in 1935 by George Allen and Unwin, and reprinted several times since); this is long, factual and behaviouristic. *A Leonard Bloomfield Anthology* (ed. C. F. Hockett. Bloomington: Indiana University Press, 1970) contains some interesting general papers on language, including Bloomfield's 1923 review of Saussure. The best entry to Chomsky (b.1928), whose writings are in part technical and difficult for the lay reader to keep up with, is by way of an annotated reader: Chomsky: *Selected Readings* (ed. J. P. B. Allen and Paul van Buren. Oxford: OUP, 1971). Two of Chomsky's own books aimed at lay readers, both highly instructive, are *Language and Mind* (revised edn New York: Harcourt Brace Jovanovich, 1972), and *Reflections on Language* (New York: Pantheon, 1975). For a clear and authoritative survey of Chomsky's ideas there is a 'Modern Master' volume, John Lyons's *Chomsky* (London: Fontana, or, in a revised edition, Hassocks: Harvester Press, 1977).

Of linguists working in the Saussurean tradition, two

seem pre-eminent. The Dane Louis Hjelmslev (1899–1965), whose *Prolegomena to a Theory of Language* can be read in English (trans. Francis J. Whitfield. Revised edn Madison: University of Wisconsin Press, 1969), and his *Essais linguistiques* in French (Paris: Editions de Minuit, 1971). And the French linguist Emile Benveniste (1902–76), in his *Problèmes de linguistique générale* (Paris: Gallimard, 1966) and *Problèmes de linguistique générale 2* (Paris: Gallimard, 1974). Also useful is André Martinet: *Elements of General Linguistics* (*Eléments de linguistique générale*, 1960. Trans. E. Palmer. London: Faber, 1960).

The influence of phonology on Structuralism can be well traced in Roman Jakobson's (1896–1982) *Six Lessons on Sound and Meaning* (*Six leçons sur le son et le sens*, 1976. Trans. John Mepham. Hassocks: Harvester Press, 1978). The book has an introduction by Lévi-Strauss, which provides interesting evidence of the direct influence of Jakobson's method of phonological analysis on his own method in anthropology. More technical and demanding is the principal work of Jakobson's foremost Russian collaborator, N. S. Troubetskoy (1890–1938): *Principles of Phonology* (trans. Baltaxe. Berkeley: University of California Press, 1969), which contains some informative addenda by way of letters written by Troubetskoy.

The work of recent or contemporary philosophers of language throws much light on the subject-matter of this book, but this literature is too large to be susceptible of itemization here. However, the first three chapters of John Passmore's *Recent Philosophers* (London: Duckworth, 1985) link Structuralism very lucidly with contemporary Anglo-American philosophy; and a valuable reader, containing major essays by both theoretical linguists and philosophers, is *The Philosophy of Linguistics* (ed. Jerrold J. Katz. Oxford: OUP, 1985).

C. SOCIAL SCIENCES

It is not necessary to follow the phenomenological influences on Structuralism very far. Edmund Husserl's

(1859–1938) major writings are complex, but two brief, fairly straightforward summaries of his thought may be found in *Husserl: Shorter Works* (ed. Peter McCormick and Frederick A. Elliston. Hassocks: Harvester Press, 1981), which contains the text of his inaugural lecture at the university of Freiburg in 1917, as well as of his article on 'Phenomenology' for the *Encyclopaedia Britannica* (1927). Some of the writings of Husserl's closest French follower, Maurice Merleau-Ponty (1908–61) are helpful, notably certain essays in *In Praise of Philosophy* (*Eloge de la philosophie*, 1960. Trans. J. Wild and J. M. Edie. Evanston, Ill.: Northwestern University Press, 1963) and *Signes* (Paris: Gallimard, 1961). A reasonably plain and highly authoritative guide to Gestalt Psychology, the other, linked German influence on Structuralist thought, is Wolfgang Köhler's *Gestalt Psychology* (New York: Liveright, 1947).

Structuralist anthropology has been dominated by the writings of Claude Lévi-Strauss (b.1908), which are numerous. Essential are *Structural Anthropology* (*Anthopologie structurale*, 1960. Trans. C. Jacobson and B. Grundfest Schoepf. London: Allen Lane, 1968); his largely autobiographical volume *Tristes tropiques* (*Tristes tropiques*, 1955. Trans. John and Doreen Weightman. London: Jonathan Cape, 1973) and *The Savage Mind* (*La Pensée sauvage*, 1962. London: Weidenfeld and Nicolson, 1966). There are most illuminating essays also in *Structural Anthropology Volume 2* (*Anthropologie structurale 2*, 1973. New York: Basic Books, 1976) and in *The View from Afar* (*Le Regard éloigné: Anthropologie structurale 3*, 1983. Trans. J. Neugroschel and P. Hoss. Oxford: Blackwell, 1985). The four large volumes of Lévi-Strauss's *Mythologiques*, dealing with the corpus of Amerindian myths, have all been translated into English (published in London by Cape). They are specialized but an impressive example of Structuralism at work. The introduction to the first volume, *The Raw and the Cooked* (1970), and the postscript to the last, *The Naked Man* (1981), are particularly illuminating on Lévi-Strauss's method and philosophical views. For an assessment of his contribution by a fellow anthropologist: E. R. Leach's *Lévi-Strauss* in the 'Modern Master' series (London: Fontana, 1974). *The Structural Study of Myth and Totemism* (ed. E. R. Leach. London: Tavistock, 1974) contains essays by a number of eminent anthropologists plus a translation of Lévi-Strauss's celebrated analysis of 'The Story of Asdiwal'.

The application of Structuralist methods in the writing of history is a subject weightily and incisively discussed in Fernand Braudel's (1902–85) *On History* (*Ecrits sur l'histoire*, 1969. Trans. S. Matthews. London: Weidenfeld and Nicolson 1980). Similarly, there is much to be learnt from the essays in Emmanuel le Roy Ladurie: *The Territory of the Historian* (*Le Territoire de l'historien*, 1973. Trans. Ben and Siân Reynolds. Hassocks: Harvester Press, 1979), or in *Modern European Intellectual History: Reappraisals and New Perspectives* (ed. Dominick LaCapra and Steven L. Kaplan. Ithaca, NY: Cornell University Press, 1982). The three volumes of *Faire de l'histoire* (ed. Jacques le Goff and Pierre Nora. Paris: Gallimard, 1974) contain some splendid and germane surveys of the 'new' history associated with Structuralism. Of the writings of Michel Foucault (1926–84), the relevant ones from a Structuralist point of view are *The Order of Things: An Archaeology of the Human Sciences* (*Les Mots et les choses*, 1966. Trans. A. M. Sheridan Smith. London: Tavistock, 1974) and *The Archaeology of Knowledge* (*L'Archéologie du savoir*, 1969, plus *l'Ordre du discours*, 1971. Trans. A. M. Sheridan Smith. London: Tavistock, 1972). There is also a useful collection of Foucault's essays in translation: *Language, Counter-Memory, Practice*. (Trans. Donald F. Bouchard and Sherry Simon. Oxford: Blackwell, 1977).

D. SEMIOTICS

The classical texts in Semiotics are contained in the writings of the American philosopher C. S. Peirce (1839–1914). The main ones can be found in Volume 2 of his *Collected Papers* (ed. Charles Hartshorne and Paul Weiss. Harvard

University Press, 1978). Peirce's most prominent American follower was Charles Morris (1901–79), whose work in Semiotics is brought together in *Writings on the General Theory of Signs* (The Hague: Mouton, 1971). The leading European writer on the subject has been the Italian Umberto Eco (b. 1932). His *A Theory of Semiotics* (*Trattato di semiotica generale*, 1975. Bloomington and London: Indiana University Press, 1975) gives a detailed and expert account. More recently he has published, directly in English, *Semiotics and the Philosophy of Language* (Bloomington: Indiana University Press, 1984). A more idiosyncratic writer on Semiotics was Roland Barthes (1915–80), in his *Elements of Semiology* (*Eléments de sémiologie*, 1964. Trans. A. Lavers and C. Smith. London: Jonathan Cape, 1967), *The Fashion System* (*Système de la mode*, 1967. Trans. London: Jonathan Cape, 1984), which analyses the language in which fashion journals describe clothes, and above all in his *Mythologies* (*Mythologies*, 1957. Trans. A. Lavers. London: Jonathan Cape, 1972. N.B. This English translation is incomplete, several of the original essays having been omitted.)

Other guides to Semiotics that can be read in English are Pierre Guiraud: *Semiology* (*La sémiologie*, 1971. London: Routledge and Kegan Paul, 1975), and *The Tell-Tale Sign: A Survey of Semiotics* (ed. Thomas A. Sebeok. Lisse, Netherlands: Peter de Ridder Press, 1975). In French there are some useful studies: Jeanne Martinet's *Clefs pour la sémiologie* (Paris: Seghers, 1973); Georges Mounin's *Introduction à la sémiologie* (Paris: Minuit, 1970); and Luis J. Prieto's contribution on 'La sémiologie' to *Le Langage* (ed. A. Martinet. Encyclopédie de la Pléiade. Paris: Gallimard, 1968).

The semiotic aspects of psychoanalysis quickly become apparent in reading Freud's more general statements of his method, as in *Beyond the Pleasure Principle* (Trans. C. J. M. Hubback. London: Hogarth Press, 1942), or the *Introductory Lectures on Psychoanalysis* (trans. Joan Riviere. London: George Allen and Unwin, 1922); or, best of all, the methodological sections of *The Interpretation of Dreams* (trans.

James Strachey. London: George Allen and Unwin, 1954). The writings of Freud's subtlest and most ambitious French interpreter, Jacques Lacan (1901–81) are notoriously difficult. A selection of his essays has appeared in English as *Ecrits: A Selection (Ecrits*, 1967. Trans. Alan Sheridan. London: Tavistock, 1977. The English volume is, as the subtitle indicates, a translation of only some of the essays contained in the French volume of the same name). Also available and more accessible is *The Four Fundamental Concepts of Psychoanalysis (Le Séminaire, Livre XI*, 1973. Trans. Alan Sheridan. London: Hogarth Press, 1977).

E. LITERATURE

Russian Formalism. There is no ideal anthology in English as yet of the writings of the Formalists, but *Readings in Russian Poetics* (ed. L. Matejka and K. Pomorska. Cambridge, Mass: MIT Press, 1971) is extremely useful. It overlaps surprisingly little with its French equivalent: *Théorie de la littérature* (ed. Tzvetan Todorov. Paris: Seuil, 1965). There is a full and informative account of the movement in Victor Erlich's *Russian Formalism: History, Doctrine* (New Haven and London: Yale University Press, 1981). The one longer example of Formalist work which should be consulted is Vladimir Propp's *Morphology of the Folktale* (*Morfologija skazki*, 1928. Austin: University of Texas Press, 1968).

To understand the transition from Formalism to full-blown literary Structuralism, a fine starting-point is the incisive critique of Formalist method in Mikhail Bakhtin and P. M. Medvedev's *The Formal Method in Literary Scholarship* (*Formal'nyi metod v literaturovedenii*, 1928. Trans. Albert J. Wehrle. Baltimore: Johns Hopkins University Press, 1978). Of Bakhtin's (1895–1975) other writings, perhaps the most useful and enlightening from a Structuralist point of view is the long essay on 'Discourse in the Novel' to be found in *The Dialogic Imagination (Voprosy literatury i estetiki*. Trans. C. Emerson and Michael Holquist. Austin and

London: University of Texas Press, 1981). A clear and comprehensive account of Bakhtin's work can be found in Tzvetan Todorov's *Mikhail Bakhtin: The dialogical principle* (*Mikhail Bakhtin: Le principe dialogique*, 1981. Trans. Wlad Godzich. Manchester University Press, 1984.) The work of the Prague School, which was very influential in the development of literary Structuralism in the 1930s, is admirably described in F. W. Galan's *Historic Structures: The Prague School Project 1928–1946* (London: Croom Helm, 1985). There is as yet in English no adequate collection of Roman Jakobson's essays in literary theory. His major pronouncement on 'Linguistics and Poetics' appears in *Style in Language* (ed. Thomas A. Sebeok. Cambridge, Mass: MIT Press, 1960), and there is a thin selection of literary and linguistic essays in *Verbal Art, Verbal Sign, Verbal Time* (ed. K. Pomorska and S. Rudy. Oxford: Blackwell, 1985). Most of his work on literature is contained in Volumes 2 and 3 of his *Selected Writings* (The Hague: Mouton, 1971 and 1981 respectively). There is an attractive mixture of personal reminiscence and theorizing in *Dialogues between Roman Jakobson and Krystyna Pomorska* (trans. Christian Hubert. Cambridge: CUP, 1983).

As general surveys of literary Structuralism two American works stand out: Robert Scholes's *Structuralism in Literature: An Introduction* (New Haven and London: Yale University Press, 1974); and Jonathan Culler's *Structuralist Poetics: Structuralism, Linguistics and the Study of Literature* (London: Routledge and Kegan Paul, 1975). There are good essays, both for and against Structuralism, in *Approaches to Poetics* (ed. Seymour Chatman. New York: Columbia University Press, 1973).

On the French side, the writings of Roland Barthes are central, especially his *Critical Essays* (*Essais critiques*, 1964. Trans. Richard Howard. Evanston, Ill.: Northwestern University Press, 1972); *Critique et vérité* (Paris; Seuil, 1966); 'Introduction to the Structural Analysis of Narratives' in *Image, Music, Text* (ed. and trans. Stephen Heath. London: Fontana, 1977); and *S/Z* (*S/Z*, 1970. Trans. Richard Miller.

London: Jonathan Cape, 1975). There is a good 'Modern Master' volume on Barthes by Jonathan Culler (London: Fontana, 1983). A splendid short guide to its subject is Tzvetan Todorov's *Poetics* (*Poétique*, 1968. Trans. Richard Howard. Minneapolis: University of Minnesota Press, 1981). The same author's *The Poetics of Prose* (*Poétique de la prose*, 1971. Trans. Richard Howard. Ithaca, NY: Cornell University Press, 1977) is also most helpful. Another French poeticist whose work is always highly instructive is Gérard Genette. The only one of his books so far translated is *Narrative Discourse* (*Figures 3*, 1972. Trans. Jane Lewin. Ithaca, NY: Cornell University Press, 1980). Genette's *Figures 1* and *2* (Paris: Seuil, 1966 and 1969 respectively) are also well worth attention. The third French writer in this field who has contributed much to Structuralist theory is A. J. Greimas. His *Structural Semantics* (*Sémantique structurale*, 1966. Trans. D. McDowell and others. Lincoln and London: University of Nebraska Press, 1983) is difficult but in the end rewarding. The essence of Greimas's thought can be found in the two volumes of papers he has published as *Du sens* (Paris: Seuil, 1970) and *Du sens 2* (Paris: Seuil, 1983).

Finally, two especially acute surveys of contemporary literary critical thought, which put Structuralism into perspective: Frank Lentricchia's *After the New Criticism* (London: Athlone Press, 1980) and William Ray's *Literary Meaning: From Phenomenology to Deconstruction* (Oxford: Blackwell, 1984).

F. POST-STRUCTURALISM

This subject could almost be said to begin and end with the writings of Jacques Derrida (b.1930), and in particular his earlier work. The best place to start is *Speech and Phenomena, and Other Essays on Husserl's Theory of Signs* (a translation of *La Voix et le phénomène*, 1967, together with two other texts, one of them Derrida's crucial essay called 'La différance'. Trans. David B. Allison. Evanston, Ill.:

Northwestern University Press, 1973). *Of Grammatology* (*De la grammatologie*, 1967. Trans. G. Spivak. Baltimore: Johns Hopkins University Press, 1976) contains some of Derrida's most influential work, notably his long essay on Saussure. There is much to be learned also from *Writing and Difference* (*L'Ecriture et la différence*, 1967. Trans. Alan Bass. London: Routledge and Kegan Paul, 1978). Derrida's writings of the late 1970s and 1980s are more for those who have developed a taste for them and a capacity to follow him through some very labyrinthine prose.

Of critics writing in English in a post-Structuralist vein, the outstanding figure was Paul de Man (1919–84); his work is finely exemplified in many of the essays in *Blindness and Insight: Essays in the Rhetoric of Contemporary Criticism* (revised edn London: Methuen, 1983). His Yale colleague Geoffrey Hartman (b. 1930) is another much influenced by Derrida and by post-Structuralism – see especially *Criticism in the Wilderness: The Study of Literature Today* (New Haven and London: Yale University Press, 1980).

Two good, lucid accounts of the subject-matter of this chapter are: Jonathan Culler's *On Deconstruction: Theory and Criticism after Structuralism* (London: Routledge and Kegan Paul, 1983); and Christopher Norris's *Deconstruction: Theory and Practice* (London: Methuen, 1982).

INDEX

Philosophy/Religion in Paladin Books

Mythologies £2.50 ☐
Roland Barthes
An entertaining and elating introduction to the science of semiology
– the study of the signs and signals through which society expresses
itself – from the leading intellectual star.

Infinity and the Mind £3.50 ☐
Rudy Rucker
In the wake of **Gödel, Escher, Bach** comes this exceptional book
which draws from a staggering variety of source material to explore
the concept of infinity and its effect on our understanding of the
universe.

Confucius and Confucianism £2.95 ☐
D Howard Smith
A skillful and thoroughgoing study which illuminates the man and
his influence and the doctrines of Confucian thought.

Paladin Movements and Ideas Series
Series editor Justin Wintle
The series aims to provide clear and stimulating surveys of the ideas
and cultural movements that have dominated history. The first three
volumes are:

Rationalism £2.50 ☐
John Cottingham

Darwinian Evolution £2.50 ☐
Antony Flew

Expressionism £2.50 ☐
Roger Cardinal

To order direct from the publisher just tick the titles you want
and fill in the order form. PAL13082

History in Paladin Books

Europe's Inner Demons   £1.75   ☐
Norman Cohn
The history of the vilification of minority groups as scapegoats, by the author of *The Pursuit of the Millennium.*

England in the Age of Hogarth   £1.50   ☐
Derek Jarrett
An absorbing history which effectively debunks the traditionally cosy view of the eighteenth century as an age of elegance and freedom.

The War of the Flea   £1.95   ☐
Robert Taber
An authoritative study of Guerrilla warfare, theory and practice from Mao Tse-Tung to General Grivas and Che Guevara.

The Rosicrucian Enlightenment   £1.50   ☐
Frances A Yates
The Rosicrucians stood midway between the Dark Ages and the scientific Renaissance: the Hermetic tradition of magic, alchemy and the Kabbalah revealed.

A History of the Great War 1914-1918   £3.95   ☐
C R M F Cruttwell
An intelligent and graphically readable account of the campaignings and battles of the 1914-18 War presented here for the general reader along with sympathetic portraits of the leaders and generals of all the countries involved. Scrupulously fair, praising and blaming friend and enemy as circumstances demand, it has become established as the classic account of the first world-wide war. Illustrated.

Anatomy of the SS State   £2.50   ☐
Helmut Krausnick and Martin Broszat
The inside story of the concentration camps, 'probably the most impressive work on the Nazi period ever to appear'. *Times Educational Supplement.*

To order direct from the publisher just tick the titles you want
and fill in the order form.   **PAL7182**

All these books are available at your local bookshop or newsagent, or can be ordered direct from the publisher.

To order direct from the publishers just tick the titles you want and fill in the form below.

Name _____

Address _____

_____

Send to:
Paladin Cash Sales
PO Box 11, Falmouth, Cornwall TR10 9EN.

Please enclose remittance to the value of the cover price plus:

UK 45p for the first book, 20p for the second book plus 14p per copy for each additional book ordered to a maximum charge of £1.63.

BFPO and Eire 45p for the first book, 20p for the second book plus 14p per copy for the next 7 books, thereafter 8p per book.

Overseas 75p for the first book and 21p for each additional book.

Paladin Books reserve the right to show new retail prices on covers, which may differ from those previously advertised in the text or elsewhere.